One Thought
Changes Everything

One Thought
Changes Everything

MARA GLEASON

ISBN: 1545323887
ISBN 13: 9781545323885

Contents

Introduction

When I was 20 years old and a junior in college, I decided to do a semester abroad in Buenos Aires, Argentina. It was 2003, and Argentina was emerging from a horrible economic crash and a period of great instability. My parents urged me to pick another place to study abroad, as they were concerned about how dangerous Buenos Aires might be. The news reports about riots and people being forced to trade food and services in the streets because their bank accounts had vanished overnight were not exactly comforting to my parents.

"What about Dublin?" they said. "You've always wanted to go to Dublin."

I dug in my heels and insisted that I wanted to become fluent in Spanish and that it would be a fascinating time to go live in a place like Argentina. I wanted a whole new cultural experience, and Ireland seemed entirely too "safe" a choice.

Well, I got my way -- and I most certainly did not end up taking the safe path.

I didn't tell my parents until almost six years later, but within three weeks of starting my seven-month study abroad program in Buenos Aires, I was held up at gunpoint. I'm going to relay what happened to me that night: not for shock value, but because it revealed something to me about the nature of human existence that I only fully came to understand many years later, when I started to learn about an understanding of the mind referred to as "the three principles" that I describe in this book. That night taught me a truth about what we humans are made of, which is now the truth I help others uncover in themselves (and in a much less dangerous and dramatic way). To be honest, I couldn't really understand or describe what happened to me that night in Argentina until I learned about the principles behind the human experience a few years later.

Two new girlfriends from my exchange program and I planned to go to a restaurant and then to a tango bar in a cool neighborhood of Buenos Aires called Palermo Viejo. It was similar to areas of Brooklyn, New York. Only a couple years earlier, it was gritty and off limits, but it had become hip; all the 20-somethings liked to hang out there after dark. Perhaps (or obviously) naively, the three of us felt relatively safe walking around the area, as we were surrounded by other people. There were certainly much more dangerous areas of the city. Anyway, I don't remember feeling especially on guard.

One Thought Changes Everything

After dinner, we set off for the tango bar, which included walking down a quieter street without any restaurants. About halfway down that block, out of nowhere we were cut off by two guys on a motorbike. Because the three of us would've been smushed too tightly for the width of the sidewalk, I was walking a teensy bit ahead of the other two girls, so I stuck out just a hair ahead of them. That hair was the difference that led me to have a profound out-of-body experience, as opposed to just getting spooked and running away ... as my two friends did.

When the two guys on the motorbike hopped up on the sidewalk in front of us, the man on the back jumped off and grabbed me on my arm – by my upper bicep, to be exact. My girlfriends were able to escape before either of the guys could grab hold of them. In telling this story, I have often been asked about what happened to the two girls. Why did they leave me? Did we ever talk about the incident later? All I can say is, I don't know. Maybe I would have run away, too, if no one had grabbed my arm. And because I am still here today and the experience actually ended up being quite amazing, I never felt the need to ask them, "Why did you leave me there?" It seemed much simpler to just go on being friends with them and leave the incident behind us.

Once the man had my arm firmly in his grip, he reached down his pants, and I distinctly remember the last couple of "Mara" thoughts I had (meaning the familiar, in-my-body recognizable voice I know all to well) were, "Ughhhhhh, seriously?! He's going to pull his dick out?!" I felt a wave of fear and disappointment, as I figured, "OK, he's either going to expose himself to me or full-on try to rape me. This is not going to be good."

But before I could even finish following that train of thought in that familiar "Mara" tone of voice, I felt the cold metal tip of a gun against my temple. And the last thought I had was, "That's not his dick he just pulled out of his pants. That's a gun."

And then, the world went silent.

That voice that was always yip-yapping in my head just shut up: the one that is constantly chit-chatting about where to go and what to do; asking how I am feeling, how do I look, what do I want to talk about, what's next in life, yada yada, so on and so forth, all day long. It just stopped. It was as if somehow, it knew something. I say "it," because in that moment, I felt myself go away, and some bigger intelligence kicked in that knew more than I did. It understood that Mara's little yip-yapper was irrelevant. There was nothing in the realm of *me* that had any knowledge of how to deal with this situation. So without intentionally doing it, I simply shut up and got out of the way. Or *it*, that larger intelligence, knew to put me to the side, much like you would push a clueless, distracted pedestrian out of the way of an oncoming bus to save their life. All of my thoughts, all the noise that usually makes up the mind and the identity of Mara Gleason, went quiet.

In that silence, something amazing occurred. I will try to describe it, but I'm going to fall short. Words cannot capture it. You see, now I'm back in my little yip-yapping Mara mind, trying to describe something that was far beyond the littleness of me. So please forgive me if it sounds silly or trite. I'll do my best to be honest and clear about what occurred with the language I have, but the experience was truly beyond me.

When my head fell silent upon feeling that gun against my temple, the sensation that emerged in the silence was indescribably huge, like a wave of vast energy. Not the *personal* energy that makes us feel revved up, but pure, impersonal energy. Beautifully quiet. The buzzing, raw force behind life, like a kind of super knowing. Not a brain knowing, but a much bigger spiritual knowing. Without the separateness of my "Mara" thinking, I was merely an energetic experience connected to the fabric of all energy: not an individual drop, but the whole ocean. I was not raised in a religious or even particularly spiritual home, but I knew that what I was experiencing was the definition of *a power greater than oneself.* Because my *self,* driven by my normal thinking, was gone.

Yet there were small glimpses of little, personal "Mara" thoughts that came to me. Like a "Whoa!" that popped in as I realized I was looking at the gunman's hand on my arm, but I couldn't distinguish a physical end to my body and a start to his. Everything blended together. Then, when I looked beyond him to a tree that was growing out of the sidewalk, I couldn't really separate this singular blob of energy that was he and I, from the tree. Again, no end and no beginning: just one continuous flow. And then I vaguely remembered that when he originally put the gun to my temple, he'd said "Dame tu billetera." ("Give me your wallet.") I had not made a move to find my wallet, as I was too absorbed in this experience of one, continuous energy.

What was perhaps the most surprising and lovely aspect of that oneness was that I felt an enormously profound love for the man holding my arm and a gun at my head. Not the kind of love we normally think of, like the love we have for our romantic partners or our family. But rather, a deeply impersonal love that goes beyond our separate selves, our ideas, our preferences, our expectations: a much more universal love. Something that could only come through silence.

As I was having this experience, which I would describe as an "out-of-body" experience, he, my mugger, began to have it, too. How do I know? I just know. Because for a moment, he and I were the same. I was in him and he was in me. We were one. As well as the tree and everything else, I suppose. I recall feeling completely confident and at peace. Whether he shot me then and there, or whether I walked away and kept living my little Mara existence, I knew that there was a greater intelligence behind life and there was no real *end* or *beginning*.

And then, a thought came through. I felt a wave of fear wash over him (or us?), and I opened my mouth to speak the only words I would say to him during the entire experience. I said, "You're scared, and that's OK." I do not remember if I spoke the words in English or Spanish, nor do I know if I spoke them out loud or just "energetically" (believe me, even I don't know what that means, but I'm telling it exactly as it happened). And really, I don't know if I was speaking to him or to me -- or if that bigger *it* was saying it to both of us. Was that a comment on that moment, or a larger comment on the experience of life? After the words were said, he looked into my eyes, and his whole body softened. We exchanged a moment of knowing, of acknowledging what had just happened. And then, I gave him his hand back. I took it from my bicep and put it back down alongside his body. Then I turned and walked away.

After a few slow steps, I picked up the pace and started running down the sidewalk. Heading back in the direction of bars and restaurants, I remember having a loud, clear "Mara" thought come back into my head: the first one, it seemed, in a very long time: "You should go into a place with people." I caught up to my friends, and panting, I walked with them into the first bar we came across. Funnily enough, it was named Diablo.

And then it all came back.

Once I was inside the doors and could see the safety of other people sitting and chatting, all of a sudden all of my "Mara" noise came flooding back into my head. It was like a marching band coming down the street, and my mind quickly went from total silence to loud, blaring, clashing, banging noise. That feeling of vastness, peace, love and total knowing had vanished, and I became horribly uncomfortable, terrified and doubtful as I heard that voice in my head start yelling at me: "What the hell just happened?! Why didn't you just give him your wallet? Holy shit, that was scary!!" My heart was racing, my head was swimming and I thought I might pass out. I also remember feeling incredibly tight inside my body, like I'd gained a lot of weight and tried to put on a tiny pair of jeans.

But within seconds of having that anxious voice screaming at me in my head, I suddenly thought, "Wait a second. STOP! Stop it, Mara! That wasn't scary. Why are you scaring yourself right now? You're fine. You're alive. You're not in danger. And actually, that was an incredibly beautiful experience. That was the most 'safe' you've ever felt in your life. Not in a personal way, but in a spiritual way. You were just an energy and for once, there was nothing to be afraid of. And now you're just scaring yourself with all of your thinking." In that moment, I realized that you could only feel fear through thought, that you could only feel separate or alone through thought.

But for thought, we are OK. Truly, deeply OK.

I calmed down again and realized that I was just a girl standing in a bar with her friends.

After a brief exchange of, "Are you OK?" "Yeah, you? Yikes, that was so crazy. I'm glad we're OK," we ordered a round of beers and carried on – for the rest of the night and the rest of the semester.

The next day, I tried to explain the experience over the phone to my boyfriend who was back in New York, but he didn't get it. All he said was, "What?! Are you fucking crazy?! Why didn't you just give him your wallet?!" I tried to explain that what happened was not in my control. It wasn't something I did on purpose, but after a few moments I gave up. I couldn't explain my experience, and frankly didn't even understand it myself, so I tucked it away.

I remember feeling sad that I couldn't explain that huge, impersonal love I'd felt, and that I'd never come close to feeling love like that anywhere in my life. Even today, when I share the story with clients, they try to explain it away according to their personal experiences, citing things like "Oh, that's just adrenaline," or "Well, you're lucky that guy didn't just pull the trigger." It's understandable that people have that response, and I probably would have, too, had I not experienced it firsthand, but they've missed the point.

I've had adrenaline rush through me many times in my life, and that's not what happened to me. I've been bungee jumping and skydiving. I've been woken in the middle of the night by the burglar alarm while staying at my house alone. That's adrenaline. It's a far more personal experience in the head and body, and your thoughts go crazy. This was wholly different: beyond me or my body, and it seemed to emerge as a default when my thinking became almost nonexistent.

Yes, I am lucky he didn't pull the trigger, and I am certainly happy to still be alive today. Yet I hesitate to even say this, as it can so easily be misinterpreted as arrogance or bravado: I don't think it's luck or coincidence that kept him from pulling the trigger. I think something profoundly transcendent occurred that made that outcome obsolete. For a brief moment, he and I experienced a oneness and an impersonal love that made any action such as pulling a trigger a non option. Temporarily, we were not separated by our thoughts. We were the formless energy of life having a shared experience. Everything was perfectly … OK. And it was beautiful beyond words.

Part One

THREE SIMPLE PRINCIPLES

One

How Did I Get Involved in This Work?

"This makes life make sense."

- Me

That night in Buenos Aires was a foreshadowing of something I was later going to discover in simpler, less dramatic terms about the nature of life. Although I didn't know it at the time, that profound experience was a taste of what I would end up devoting my life's work to. What I came to discover in my journey of learning about the three principles of *mind, consciousness and thought,* which you'll read about in the following pages, is that all of human experience is a personalized, thought-divided experience of an underlying, impersonal energy that connects all of us. The more ... and more ... and MORE thinking we run through our system, the more separate, noisy, burdened and individualized our experience gets. And for many of us, the older we get, the more we define ourselves by our thinking and the more tightly we tend to hold onto our thinking. This "holding on" is the root of all human psychological suffering, like stress, depression, isolation and so on. On the flip side, experiences of peace of mind, flow, freshness and insight visit people when their thinking is quieter, less prominent, less important, less divisive. For a brief, but massively expanded, moment on that sidewalk in Buenos Aires, I was able to feel what exists beyond thought. When our mind goes quiet, we feel the energy behind life without the fragmentation and personalization of thoughts. In that silence lies a spiritual universal truth. We are all one. We are all OK. Only your thinking can tell you otherwise.

But don't worry. We don't need to live life as if there's a gun to our head in order to feel OK. In fact, we don't even have to *quiet the mind* intentionally with tricks and techniques, like meditation, breathing exercises and yoga. You don't even need to think of yourself as a "spiritual" person to grasp the principles discussed in this book. What you'll discover in the following pages is that by simply *understanding* that there are principles behind the human experience, one begins to understand that we aren't living in the situations and reality that we *think* we are living in. We are not dealing with what we think we're dealing with. We are dealing with the fact *that we think.* A new understanding of the mind and how it creates our experience shows us that we are only ever in a thought-created experience, and therefore, we are only ever one thought away from a whole new reality. Knowing this fundamental human truth brings about a freedom of mind that has far-reaching implications for business productivity, family relationships, athletic performance and the overall well-being of the human race. I know it sounds too good to be true, but the following chapters are the proof. If I hadn't stumbled down this path in the way I did, I probably wouldn't have believed it, either. In fact, this path, unbeknownst to me, started many years before my experience in Buenos Aires.

I know from my experience working with clients over the last 10 years that many of you reading this book are already getting impatient wanting to know exactly what "the three principles" are and why they're so important. But like I said, I don't know that I would have even *listened* to someone talk to me about the three principles if I hadn't come across them in the personally compelling way that I did. So be patient, and let me begin at the beginning. I'll tell you how I came across the principles, and then I'll tell you what the three principles are. If you're *really* impatient, feel free to skip to the next chapter and then come back to this one, if you must.

When I was 11 years old, my dad went on a business trip. He worked as the vice president of a billboard company that had several markets throughout the United States, so he was always going on business trips – which was fine by me, because when he was home, there was a palpable cloud of tension in the house that didn't exist when it was just my mom and us three kids. My dad had an intensity that could terrorize a fly. His business trips were like little vacations for us. We didn't have to frantically clean up after ourselves. We didn't have to walk around on eggshells waiting to screw up. We could be spontaneous. We didn't have to worry about getting yelled at, criticized or interrogated, and best of all, we got to see my mother relax. We didn't have to watch him put her down at the dinner table. I didn't have to go comfort her after dinner while she cried silently in the laundry room, pretending to fold clothes.

As a kid, I was angry because I didn't know which was more painful, hating my father or hating that I hated my father. I *really* wanted to be his friend and to love him, but every time I did that, I found myself feeling betrayed or stupid, like it was some naïve trap I'd been lured into again. You see, he could make you feel so incredible, like there was this special world that he commandeered that was cooler than everyone else's world, like everyone else was just a boring schmo, following all the stupid rules, and you and he were rebel cowboys that had untouchable, superior fun. He used to love to say, "There are no rules in life, only preferences" – as you and he broke some clear societal rule together. We often broke rules while proudly standing in front of the very signs where rules were posted. Like the time he and I ate take-out soup next to a sign on a boat that read, "No food allowed," me looking sheepish, while my dad wore a huge grin. He also once argued aggressively with an awkward teenager who was just trying to do his job to get me on a rollercoaster at an amusement park when I was clearly below the height requirement. I'm pretty sure those height requirements are there for a reason, but my dad was uninterested. We were going on that ride, goddammit! I was always horrified and tickled at the same time by our blatant rebelliousness. Though rare and fleeting, when you were on the inside of his special world, you and he were better than everyone else on earth. And damn, was it fun! So when you suddenly found yourself on the outside again, it was jarring to realize that your partner in crime had abruptly turned on you and become your enemy. In an instant, he'd snap and become one of the scariest people you'd ever seen. As a child, I never understood why he flared up so dramatically and so often, but the long and short of it is that for the first decade of my life I thought my dad was unpredictably terrifying and that things were nicer when he wasn't around, so I predominantly suffered when he was home.

Consequently, it was surprising when he came home from one of his business trips a different person.

He'd only been gone for four or five days. He'd left home as his usual self, and I expected him to come home his usual self. But he didn't. He walked in the house that evening, and he asked to speak to my older brother and me in the living room. (We are significantly older than our younger sister, so she was not included in this conversation, as she was three years old at the time.)

The request to speak to us instantly terrified me. Anytime my dad asked *to speak to me* in a formal manner, it meant that I'd done something wrong, and I was gonna hear about it. But to my surprise, we sat down with him, and for a good, long while I didn't hear anything. Not a word. He sat there, staring at something invisible on the floor. He was obviously choosing his words, but he seemed to be speechless for the first time in my life. When he finally looked up at us, I saw that he had tears in his eyes. This was a first for me, and it literally knocked the wind out of my chest. Here was the toughest, meanest guy I knew, tearing up for some completely unidentifiable reason. I had never seen my father cry before.

Finally, he said, through trembles, "I'm sorry. I'm sorry for the way things have been. I want things to be different. I swore I'd never be like my father …" At this point, he broke down. "… And look what I'm doing. You're terrified of me."

At that moment, I dropped into a kind of pain that I'd never experienced before in my eleven short years of life. I finally got what I thought I wanted, which was recognition from my father of how much pain he'd inflicted upon us, and I instantly wanted to vomit. I immediately felt guilty and wanted to reassure him that it wasn't true: that he'd actually been a wonderful, loving father and that we thought only good things of him. But obviously, I couldn't. So I watched him cry, with no reassurances to give him other than the tears I had streaming down my own face.

As I watched him struggle for breath and words, I realized how much more deeply painful it is to watch someone you thought of as invincible experience shattering pain and guilt. I much preferred experiencing my own suffering to watching his. It felt simpler. Predictable. Eleven-year olds are supposed to feel sorry for themselves. But this powerful, grown man looking so pathetic was utterly confounding and seemingly impossible to correct. I desperately wanted the world to return to its natural order.

One Thought Changes Everything

I remember wondering to myself, "What the hell happened to this man? Did he almost die on the plane home and have an epiphany as he saw his precious life ending? Had he been captured by drug lords and held hostage in a prison for several days and forced to ponder the meaning of his life and his relationships with those he loved? Or did he finally meet his match? Someone as tough and critical as he was, who just spat the truth out in his face? Told him he was a monster of a father and needed to march home and apologize to his kids? Did my mother threaten to leave him (and actually mean it this time)? What could possibly explain this wholly different man sitting before me?"

Well, I'll tell you one thing: I wasn't about to ask. I was physically incapable of speaking in that moment. The small boulder that was lodged in my throat and the hiccups of breath I stole in between tears really weren't conducive to throwing out inquisitive remarks. So I sat there doing what I did best in the presence of my father. I shut up and listened.

After these few, but seemingly endless, minutes in which my father cried in front of us, he finished by saying, "I want things to be different from now on. I've learned some things this week, and I think things are going to be different now." To my recollection, neither my brother nor I said anything. We just nodded, and I think we felt equally confused about what he actually meant by that statement. "OK, different would be good," I thought. But I honestly didn't believe that "different" was possible. Already, I had become hardened to the notion that people could change. I assumed that people talked about change but never actually followed through on it. But here's where the magic comes in: I was wrong. Things indeed became very different. My whole life became very different.

So what had happened to him on that business trip?

To back up a bit, my dad's boss was a bright, self-made billionaire who owned several different companies, the billboard company my father worked at being one of them.

Apparently, he had learned about a small consulting practice out in rural Washington state, called Pransky and Associates, that was teaching people a simple set of three principles, *mind, consciousness and thought*, based on the insights of a man named Sydney Banks. These principles explain how people create their experience of life via basic, internal forces, showing people that all of life experience is an inside job and that without realizing it, we have endless potential to have new thought and, thus, new experiences, completely independent of external circumstances.

I'll go into more depth about these principles in the next chapter, but the result of people learning these principles was that in a four-day educational program, people came to understand how their experience of life comes about: that it is coming *from* them, not happening *to* them (reversing many people's assumptions about life). The understanding gave them profound new insight into how we can naturally access new thoughts in any moment, and thus new experiences. It gave people the roadmap for more clarity and freedom without anything external in their life needing to change.

Even better, there was no Meyers-Briggs assessment at the beginning, no psychological or behavioral interventions, no techniques to be practiced, no "how-to" prescriptions, no 12 steps, just plain and simple education: *Here's how the human experience works. There are core principles that explain it. Your understanding of those principles leads to greater and greater levels of freedom and clarity of mind. This is where human potential lies. Now, go do whatever you want with it.*

Well, what my dad's boss decided to do with it was train the people in his company about these principles because he recognized the massive business implication in what he'd already seen for himself. Imagine people in a business operating with more clarity of mind, less stress and reactivity, and the understanding of the internal workings that determine that unrestricted capacity – completely independent of external factors. People's accountability and resiliency can skyrocket with this understanding. His boss saw that this could be a game-changer in business, especially for someone like my dad. Lucky for me!

That's where my dad went for four days. Not to a prison camp in the mountains of Colombia or aboard a crashing plane. He went to a tiny town north of Seattle and learned those three principles that I will discuss in detail throughout this book. Basically, he went to a course in how life works. The amazing thing was that it was a "business trip," yet it changed his family life. It changed *my* life. I'm not going to be ridiculous and suggest that he became *perfect* overnight. Of course not. But he became *very* different. He relaxed. He became aware of his reactivity and short temper in the moment and made internal corrections. He quit taking his stress out on the family all the time, and in truth, there was just much less stress bottled up in him. He was letting go. All because he was educated about the role his own mind was playing in life and the freedom he had to adjust his state of mind.

You could see he'd touched a quieter, more settled place in himself. Believe me, he was still no walk in the park, but he wasn't a pervasive, terrifying dark cloud – he was more of a scattered thunderstorm. And much to my surprise, the positive changes I saw not only lasted, but grew. Being the skeptical 11-year old that I was, I assumed whatever positive changes I was seeing were going to dissolve quickly. Delightfully, I was proven wrong. Over the following months and years, I got more and more of the incredible parts of my father and less and less of the difficult parts of him. I quit hating him and started loving him. Really, truly loving him.

Observing such profound change in my father is what eventually led me to pursue a career in this emerging field of *the three principles*. I decided I *must* know what he learned that led to that kind of change in such a short amount of time. Because of all people, my dad is a tough nut to crack. He's got a bullshit detector like no other, and he's not going to take advice or counseling from people. He's incredibly bright and excruciatingly picky about who and what he has the patience to listen to. You have to go deep to inspire someone like my dad, but without a trace of new-age fluffiness or institutional psycho-babble. In fact, he hates anything that's been institutionalized, including religion. As far as he's concerned, anything that takes away people's freedom of mind is for the birds. But if it's truth on offer, he'll hear it. Anything short of that, and he'll blow it off. Therefore, I knew that what he learned must have been be the real deal. It must have been true. And I wanted to know more.

Because my dad knew I was curious and had asked a lot of questions in the years since that amazing tear-filled conversation with him, sometime in the spring of my sophomore year of college he sent me a book by Sydney Banks entitled *The Enlightened Gardener*. It wasn't actually even a book yet, but rather the loose transcript. Apparently, over the years since my dad came across *the three principles* understanding, he'd had several opportunities to meet and talk with Sydney Banks, and the two had formed something of a friendship. Syd had sent my dad the transcript of his latest book-in-progress, asking for his feedback. For some fortuitous reason, my dad decided to send it to me while I was away at college in upstate New York. I remember receiving a notice in my mailbox that I had a package to pick up. Inside the large envelope, I found the loose pages of Syd's manuscript and a brief note from my dad on his office notepaper that stated, "From the Office of Kevin Gleason." My dad's scribbled words read, "To Mara. Thought you would enjoy this. Love, Dad." I was both surprised and tickled that my dad had sent me these mysterious pages. It was not a typical thing for me to receive a package from my dad. I was eager to see what he'd sent me and why he thought I'd enjoy it, so I walked out of the mailroom, on to the campus "green," as they called it, and parked myself under the nearest tree. It was a mild spring day in Saratoga Springs, so I was content to sit and read for bit outdoors before my next class began.

But funnily enough, I didn't end up going to my next class. Once I started reading Syd's book, I couldn't stop. A friend from my afternoon class passed me on the way and yelled to me, "Hey, you coming?" I looked up from my reading and paused for a second, surprised at what was coming out of my mouth. "Umm. No … not today." I had never "skipped" a class. I'd only ever missed one due to illness or travel. But for some reason, in that moment, I knew that what I was reading under that tree was more important than that class. It wasn't because it was such a gripping book or that the writing style was so magnetic. Quite the contrary. It was just so simple. What I read in Syd's *The Enlightened Gardener* explained the principles behind the human experience so clearly that I got the overwhelming, deep sensation of *this makes life make sense.* Every time I had suffered and every time I had felt joy suddenly made sense. Who I was, what I was made of and how my experience of life unfolds made plain, simple, clear sense. With this realization, I didn't feel euphoric or giddy. I felt truly and wholly at peace, and I could see that this was all anyone was ever seeking. And then, it was cemented. I knew I wanted to share these principles with the world. This was going to be my life's work.

When I graduated from college a couple of years later and moved to Washington state to do an internship with Pranksy and Associates, the place my dad had gone for four days when I was 11 years old, I was shocked to see that the seemingly freakish, dramatic change I witnessed in my father was actually happening to all kinds of people all the time, just by learning these principles. In retrospect, I realized that I had kind of assumed he was a unique case: someone who had had an *unusually* profound shift. But not surprisingly, I suppose, if these principles universally make sense of life, then surely it would help anyone and everyone. I just didn't believe it was that simple, because I was raised in a society that was so trained to think of change as slow, hard and often impossible. Yet during my four-month internship, I saw that dramatic, lasting change was the norm for people who learned these principles. I saw huge, enduring shifts in nearly every person that went through the Pranskys' program. The more I observed, the more sure I became that not only was this to be my life's work, but that this understanding has the power to change the world. It unlocks something so big in people and in such a short amount of time. It became increasingly bewildering to me and to my clients: If this understanding is so powerful -- and IT IS! -- why doesn't everyone know about this? In fact, I began to get frustrated hearing that question over and over again from my clients. At some point, almost all of my clients, whether an astrophysicist, a rabbi, or a military lieutenant, would get a puzzled look on their face and say to me, "No, really. How come this isn't mainstream? It's game-changing." That is one reason, if not the biggest reason, for my writing this book. It is also why, at 27 years old, I left Pransky and Associates in northern Washington state to co-found One Thought, with Aaron Turner. Together, we wanted to reach more people by launching a company in New York City and London to share these principles with leaders and organizations around the world. For the next six incredible years, Aaron and I spent the majority of our time traveling around the world working with businesses leaders, innovators, military leaders, educators and other leadership consultants, sharing these principles because we passionately wanted an understanding of these principles to become mainstream. We wanted everyone to know that this freedom of mind is universally available.

I never thought I would have my own company, and now my own global nonprofit, and I certainly never thought I would write a book. But here I am today, writing this book, because I feel strongly that the message contained in these pages has the potential to make the world a better place. I know people like to throw that phrase around a lot – "make the world a better place." (I think it's even in a Michael Jackson song.) But honest to goodness, it applies here. I know, because I saw the very principles I am going to illuminate in this book make my father's world a better place, which made my world a better place, and which was the impetus for me devoting my life to sharing these principles with others, because I realized what happened to him could happen to anyone.

Two

What Are the Three Principles and Why Do They Help People?

"Thought creates our world and then says, 'I didn't do it.'"

- David Bohm

The "three principles" is shorthand for the *three principles of mind, thought and consciousness,* which is a framework or a description that explains what's behind the human experience. But before I go any further, I have to start by clarifying the word "principles," because I, personally, didn't like the sound of this term when I first heard it. Truthfully, if it hadn't been for the change I observed firsthand in my father, I probably would have dismissed the whole thing. But really, my reaction to the term "principles," or anyone's reactions to anything for that matter, is based on preconceived notions of definitions of things. And my definition of the word "principles" was based on *one* of the definitions of the word, which is a *person's belief or morals.* That makes the term "principles" start to sound like something righteous, or religious, or dare I say cult-like. But really, it just sounds *personal.* The second definition of "principle" in the Oxford English Dictionary is not personal at all:

- *a fundamental source or basis of something:* the first principle of all things was water.
- a fundamental quality or attribute determining the nature of something; an essence

This second definition is what "the three principles" are pointing to: a fundamental source or basis of the human experience; an essence. *Mind, thought and consciousness* are the fundamental sources, or what I sometimes think of as fundamental *forces,* that make up the human experience. Because they are fundamental, they are universal to all human beings. Without these three components, none of us would be able to have any experience at all.

Mind is the energy that runs through all things. It is not a personal energy, but rather a universal, broader energy. *Mind* is not the same as the brain, although that energy is in the brain. It's in every cell in our body and every atom in the universe. It is bigger than any one of us, but it allows for the existence of each of us. It is what allows your heart to beat, blood to flow, and mental activity to light up your brain. *Mind* is not specific to you or concerned with what specific *kind* of heartbeat you have or the *kind* of mental activity that shows up in you, but rather the simple human energy and intelligence that allows for any of that to occur when you come alive. As long as you are living, *Mind* is an energetic potential that allows for you to have the next heartbeat, the next breath, the next thought – to turn on your experience of life.

Thought is the content that we use to create our experience of life. Without a thought, you can't have an experience. It makes all experience possible. Without thought, we can't have a self, a notion of who we are. We literally create our understanding of ourselves via thought. I know it's impossible to fully wrap our heads around this one, because we are literally in thought *all the time* from the moment we're born. So stepping back and considering that our experience comes from thought is sort of like asking a fish, "How's the water?" We're so immersed in it all the time, it's hard to step back and look at it with any broader perspective. In an attempt to state it strongly and succinctly, if you have an experience of something, it has to be in your thinking.

I'll give you a few everyday examples of how thoughts drive all experience to make it a tad more tangible. Have you ever been sitting in a business meeting or at a child's dance recital, or been driving a car and your mind drifted off? You start thinking about what you need to do later that day – *pick up your dry cleaning, buy eggs at the store, call your sister, ugh, and speaking of your sister, what is going on with her? and----I'm sorry, what?* Suddenly you realize someone in the meeting has asked you a question, and you're embarrassed to admit you have no idea what they were saying. Even though you were sitting smack in front of them, looking into their eyes, watching their mouths move, your thinking wasn't actually about what they were saying. Your thinking was about what you have to do later that day. And for those moments that your thinking was on dry cleaning and phone calls to your sister, your experience was in those activities. You could picture the dry cleaners or your sister's face, because in your mind, that's where you were. Not physically, but *experientially*. Wherever thought goes, there you go.

As another example, if I tell you to think about the saddest thing that could ever happen to you, you'll start feeling sad – even if you're sitting on the beach in the middle of a great vacation and this awful thing hasn't actually happened at all! Because thought will take you there. How many people do you know who go on vacation but stay at work in their mind? Maybe you're married to one of these people. You have the sensation that they're *not there* with you, because they're *still at work*.

People often have the same experience reading a book. Anytime you've ever had to go back and read a page over again, it's not because you somehow forgot how to read midway through the page. Your eyes were still following the words, but your thinking went elsewhere, you drifted off, got distracted, so your experience went elsewhere. Because you had no experience of the last half page, you have no idea what happened and you have to go back, so you can actually experience what's going on in the book, not just vacantly read the words.

I'll give you one more example of how our thinking creates our experience of life and actually, how many of us adults use our knowledge of that to manipulate our children's experience. You know when toddlers are running and fall down, there's often that moment where they look up at you, stunned, not sure what to make of the face-plant they just endured … so they look at you for guidance? You have a split-second window to sway their thinking one way or the other. If you smile and make light of it, they think they should do the same, and they seem to be all right. If you pause too long or you look worried and concerned, they often burst into tears. This is their thinking playing out in the moment. We can see in children that it's easy to sway their thinking, and thus we often do, preventing their experience from turning into an unpleasant or difficult one.

To reiterate, thought is behind all our experience. Without thought we *cannot have an experience*. It's as fundamental to our life experience as our heartbeat. "*I think; therefore, I am.*"

Consciousness is what brings our thinking to life and makes us *aware* of what we're thinking. It allows us to have feeling and to feel our thinking. We don't live in the feeling of an external world. We live in the feeling of our thinking. I liken it to the special effects department of the human system. Whatever thinking we have runs through our sensory system, giving us a surround-sound, high-definition experience of our thought, as if it's completely real and as if it's coming from something other than our thinking. (Remember a second ago when I told you to think of the saddest thing that could happen to you? You can create quite a powerful feeling in your body because of this interplay between thought and consciousness.)

In order to feel anything, we have to be conscious. Dreams are a fascinating demonstration of how consciousness brings our thinking to life as a feeling in our bodies. I have had dreams where I'm falling from great heights, or in a crashing plane, and I actually feel my stomach jump up into my throat. Or I have had dreams where I am running or frightened and I wake up sweating in my bed. Why? Not because I was actually running in real life, but because my body was having an *experience* of fright and exertion, simply because the thoughts I was having were brought to life as a feeling in my body, via consciousness. I often joke that consciousness is so much more powerful than the greatest Hollywood special effects team, because no matter what you think, consciousness will bring that thinking to life in your body and make it feel absolutely real.

I'll give you a visual, as that can be helpful. Many people assume that we are like cameras, walking around taking snapshots of the world *out there*. Whatever is there, our "camera" is objectively capturing it. But in truth, the mind works more like an old-fashioned film projector. From the human mind, via thought, we create a picture of life and project it out on to the screen of our experience. We live in a movie of our own making. Mind is the power source, thought is the film, and consciousness is the bulb that lights it up.

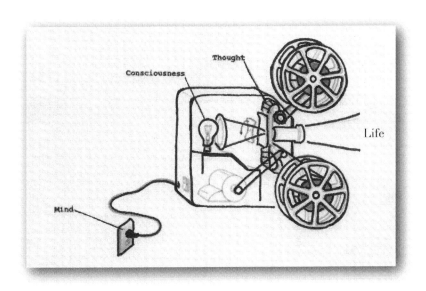

How does learning these three principles help someone? It is not the concepts or the separate definition of each principle that helps people. But rather, it's when the fluid, seamless interplay of these internal forces is *realized* by a person in moments in their life; then the principles come to life for the person. Similar to those silly *Magic Eye* 3D posters, which were very popular in the '90s, the observer has to let their eyes and all their desire to *find it* relax, and suddenly a clear image emerges from all the little bits and pieces.

It is my observation in my professional work with individuals and teams (ranging from high-level business leaders, to military, to athletes, and even people with eating disorders, addictions and psychiatric diagnoses) over the last 10 years, that when people learn that these principles are behind all human experience, two major shifts occur that are like the first couple of dominos that fall or the first 3D images to come clear, leading to a long line of subsequent changes in their life.

The first domino is the realization that 100 percent of our experience is coming from the inside-out, rather than the outside-in. There are basic, understandable, predictable, internal principles that explain how we experience life. That is incredibly powerful because it clears up a lot of misconceptions and frustrations people have when they are living life feeling like the world is happening *to* them, as opposed to coming from within. Essentially, people stop feeling at the mercy of things outside themselves, like circumstances and other people. And because consciousness makes us feel our thinking as *very compelling* and *very real*, the thought that it is the externals causing their feelings seemed like a rock solid fact … until they learn these principles. The reversal of that assumption gives people more freedom than they ever realized was possible in life.

The second domino is the realization that thought is just a transient energy. Essentially, it's not real. And it's temporary. It comes into the mind, and while it's there it seems very real and compelling, but if you don't do anything with it, it will go. (See two year-olds for a perfect example. Their experience shifts easily and effortlessly moment to moment because their thinking is very fluid. You rarely find a depressed two year-old.) Thought is much like the clouds in the sky. Clouds take different shapes and forms, and from the window of a plane, clouds can look very solid, almost like you could lie down on one of them and take a nice nap. But we all know that's not the case. You'd actually fall right through a cloud, because it's not solid. Clouds are tiny droplets of water floating through the air, coming into form and then disappearing again, just like the thoughts that run through our mind. They seem so solid while we're looking at them, but the second we look away, they disappear and turn into some other thought.

People often hear phrases that point at this truth. For example, my grandma always said, "This too shall pass." But learning that it's not just a nice-sounding phrase, it's actually a *principle* of human experience, makes our life experiences much less frightening and stressful. All experience is borne of thought, and no thought is permanent. If you give your mind the opportunity, it will self-correct. You will gravitate toward a clearer state of mind, much like if you leave a scab alone, it will heal and go away. But if you pick at it, it will get worse and bleed, and potentially leave a bigger scar. That's part of the power of *Mind*, that universal energy. It's an endless supply of thought, for as long as you're alive. Seeing that life is not *happening to us* and that it's built into the intelligence of the human system for new thoughts and new experiences to come, if we allow, gives people an enormous capacity to be less frightened by their experiences, and much more resilient in the midst of them.

What was most surprising for me, when I first began my internship learning the three principles at Pransky and Associates, was that my seemingly spiritual and inexplicable experience of being held up at gunpoint in Buenos Aires suddenly had a framework that explained it in simple terms.

I remember the exact day when I was observing a client session as an intern-in-training and it clicked: what had occurred that night in Buenos Aires made sense according to these principles. My colleague and his client were talking about how thought is like the mediator through which we experience life. It's really just an energy that takes a form in our head, and while we're in whatever form that thought takes, that's what we experience – whether it's happy thinking, sad thinking, stressed thinking, fearful thinking, what do I want to have for dinner thinking and so on. And if you turn up the volume on that thought, or hold tightly to it, it has a real presence in your experience of life. But the thinking we don't hold tightly to, or play too loudly in our minds, just glides through us, staying only briefly. It comes and it goes. And generally, the louder and tighter people's thinking gets, the more alone, frustrated and frightened they become because they feel stuck.

Yet when people's thinking is quiet or more fluid, people feel a sense of ease and a broader connection with people because their individual thoughts aren't so prominent and isolating. And they feel like there's a flow, of something *doing* life on their behalf, rather than having to personally muscle their way through life by themselves.

Suddenly a light bulb went off in my mind: *That's why I experienced a profound feeling of connectedness when he put that gun to my head. My thinking, temporarily, went quiet. So quiet it practically disappeared.* In terms of the principles of mind, consciousness and thought, it makes sense that the louder your thinking about yourself, your job, your relationship or your finances gets, the more you feel separate and burdened, because consciousness is playing that thinking out onto the screen of your life.

But without all that thinking, what's left is just *mind* – the energy behind life. The one thing that unites us. I was fortunate enough to have a brief glimpse into what life is like just beyond the filter of our thinking. It explained it all. When I walked into the bar and all my thinking came rushing back, I immediately got that overwhelming feeling of anxiety and fear. In a flash, I saw the true meaning of "there's nothing to fear but fear itself." I could now see that what limits people is not life, but all our thinking about life. And when that's not there, we are just a universal energy.

I could now understand what had happened to me in simple terms. I no longer needed to tuck it away. But even more, I could begin to share a simple understanding of how all people can have more of a sense of that feeling of connectedness, or pure "OK-ness," as I came to think of it, without having to have a gun to their head. You could actually just be sitting at your desk at work and realize that you're only ever one thought away from a feeling of "OK." But for the sheer volume of our thinking in the moment, we are all OK.

Part Two

PEOPLE'S STORIES

The remaining chapters of this book are dedicated to stories of change I have observed in people after learning the three principles and seeing those principles come to life in the moment. *(All names and identifying details have been changed to protect clients' privacy).* As I said, my clients range from Fortune 500 business leaders and teams, to military leaders, to professional athletes, to MIT-trained physicists, to artists, to prison inmates, to people with severe diagnoses or addictions. The reason I emphasize the diversity of my clients is because it proves the point that if these principles are truly principles of the human experience (a fundamental source or basis of the human experience), then they are applicable to *all* people. There are no exceptions. And in my opinion, that offers incredible hope that nothing else out there currently offers.

The realization that we have stumbled across something that's universally true and thus helpful to all humanity is radically different than the daunting 297 diagnoses currently described in the American Psychological Association's Diagnostic Manual, considered the "bible" of psychology and psychiatry. Or the countless number of approaches to business and organizational psychology: the 7 habits, the 5 dysfunctions, the 12 steps, the bajillion "laws," the endless techniques that lead to great leaders. You need only peruse the list of the top 50 business and leadership books to see what I'm referring to.

What if it was simpler than that: a single understanding that could change all of human experience, from the professional hockey player that wants to play better, to the CEO that wants to transform the culture in the company, to the dancer who wants to stop feeling imprisoned by bulimia? What if there was one answer for anyone looking to feel better or do better in life? I know it might seem outlandish, but I'm suggesting that these principles offer that answer.

The reason the part of this book about the three principles themselves is very short and the part about client stories is much longer is because client stories are a far better way to understand the *point* of the principles, and they show the breadth of application of these principles. Unfortunately, you can't grasp the principles of *mind, consciousness and thought* intellectually, because they are before the personal use of thought (i.e. the intellect). So reading them as concepts on a page doesn't necessarily do much for people. It'd be like telling a kid to make a physical representation of the universe for a science project. I remember "shoe box dioramas" were popular during my childhood in the '80s and '90s. Before kids had computers and no one was making Power Point presentations for their classes, we made our science projects out of old shoe boxes. They were like a little stage inside which we created scenes. I distinctly remember making the planets of our solar systems out of balls of aluminum foil and hanging those "planets" from the top of the box with dental floss. It was quite an impressive representation of our solar system! (I'm joking. Obviously, it looked quite pathetic and bore no actual resemblance to the sun and the planets of our solar system.) But it wasn't my little 8-year-old self's fault that I couldn't quite do our solar system justice. Where we live and what we have access to is much smaller than the solar system or the *entire* universe, and thus it's impossible for us to define it in a single structure. We are within the universe, and thus can know its existence, but we certainly can't draw four lines around it. It's far bigger than that. We can imagine it and be in awe of it, but can we really wrap our minds around the entirety of it? No. Can we have a sense of it, or a feel for it? Absolutely.

That's why I suggest that client stories are a better means for understanding the principles. You can observe the power of how understanding the principles creates change in people's lives without trying to draw four lines around it. You can simply get a feel for it. And that's where it creates change for the reader: in the feeling of it. While this may sound somewhat abstract, it's actually something human beings are already doing all the time especially when we're young and learning new things on a regular basis.

There are plenty of things we learn by feeling, not through defining them intellectually. For example, studying *mind, consciousness and thought* as concepts would be like the equivalent of studying swimming in a book about water, stroke and breathing. It can give you a surface-level, conceptual understanding of a phenomenon, but it's not until you dive into the water and feel the coolness on your skin, the weightlessness of your body, and that seemingly challenging at first, but eventually effortless ability to propel yourself through water without having to gasp for breath or jerk your muscles about too much that you really *feel* swimming. Essentially, you learn to swim by *feeling* swimming, not thinking it.

These stories are meant to be a jump in the ocean. You can get a feel for the infinite potential for change, the vastness it creates in people's experience and the undeniable truth that we are all living this energy, this potential, this magic. And when we stop jerking about, when we stop gasping for breath and essentially trying too damn hard, the feel for it just comes to us. So to put the last paragraph much more succinctly, as you read these client stories, relax and let the water carry you, and the rest of your understanding will take care of itself. You'll feel things changing without you having to do it.

Before I dive into client stories, I'll say a small bit about how I work with clients. We have a conversation. There. That's it. I've told you the whole "process." There's no PowerPoint presentation. No workbook. No graphs and statistics. Sometimes I'll draw pictures to illustrate something that we're discussing in the conversation, but not always. Whether it's an individual that I work with over four days, or a large team that I work with over three to five days, it's always just a conversation about how people experience their life or their challenges from the inside, out, and how an understanding of the internal principles of mind, consciousness, and thought shed new light on that experience. We dialogue, ask questions and share stories. It's not information being handed from teacher to student, but rather a set of principles placed on the table for us to then play with, reflect on, experiment with and see if they hold water. It's a shared experience, and it's often surprising and notable to the people I work with.

I've received comments like, "You know, the best part of this course it that there's no bells and whistles. At first, that made me uncomfortable, because I thought if it didn't look impressive, flashy or exciting, it wouldn't hold my attention. But now I feel that's been the best part. It's just a truth about life. And all truths about life hold their own. They don't need to be dressed up."

Or others have said, "I couldn't believe that the 30 of us were going to sit in a room and just *talk* for three days. That seemed way too boring. But the days flew by, and I realized that in fact, the most meaningful moments in my life have been pivotal conversations. And I just got to soak in three days' worth of that."

In the client stories you're about to read, while I don't give hour-by-hour details of what was talked about with each individual or group because of course I don't remember the specifics, you can know that it was always just a conversation about how these invisible principles can become visible in any human experience. And when they do, our challenges, our relationships and our lives suddenly make a whole lot more sense and seem full of much greater possibility. As people begin to realize that they are not experiencing the world "out there," but rather they are experiencing their own thinking that then creates a perception of the world, there's a whole new sense of freedom that comes over people. Life is no longer "happening to me," but rather "coming from me." The feeling of being *under the gun* is exposed as the illusion it's always been. There is no gun out there. Well . . . except for that one time.

Three

*"The most difficult thing to learn is
something you think you know already."*

— Jiddu Krishnamurti

I'm going to start with one of my favorite client stories. It's one of my favorites because it was one of the most challenging, but ultimately most rewarding groups I've ever worked with. The company was a large multinational aerospace company. This particular division of the company was based in England, and focused on designing a specific piece of technology, urgently needed by the military. They were a relatively large team (30 or so), consisting of highly specialized engineers and physicists. A bright group, to say the least, with degrees and resumes from many of the finest institutions and companies.

Needless to say, they could dance circles around me in most any intellectual topic of discussion. And for the first two days of their four-and-a-half-day program, they did.

First, the group was incredibly irritated by the fact that their boss had pulled them out of the office for a four-and-a-half-day program on "State of Mind." (State of Mind is a term we've often used in the business world to isolate the role of the mind in various business challenges. It's our way of highlighting the three principles in a business setting.) They couldn't possibly fathom how talking about their mind for four and a half days was actually going to help them design and execute their product faster or cheaper, which is what they cared most about. Even worse, we were inviting them to participate in the course in a manner unfamiliar to their "normal." We encouraged them to slow down their minds. Listen from a blank slate. Be reflective as opposed to analytical. For a group that was accustomed to being "on" 24/7, go-go-go, the pace of our course was like pulling the emergency brake on a racing car. It wasn't pretty. Lots of participants argued with us for the first couple of days or complained about the pace being too slow.

Two participants, in particular, really struggled: Carl and Dylan. But in the end, every last person in the course came around and began to have rich, new insights into how they were using their minds in life and at work: even Carl and Dylan.

Carl was an English man in his late 40s/early 50s. He had a mostly bald head, reddish face and glasses. He also had that "geeky professor" look and was always bursting at the seams, or more literally at the cranium, with something he *had* to interject. There was always some fact, or some theory, or a contradicting argument that just fell out of his mouth. While he was often polite enough to raise his hand, he ultimately overrode the raised-hand politeness by just beginning to talk at the same time his arm started going up. "Can I say something? I'd like to add to that. … Well, actually, there's another theory about that … ." I'm not exaggerating when I say that we literally couldn't speak more than two or three sentences before Carl would have to spit something out again (in fact, spit often accompanied his words, and little bits of spittle would build up in the corners of his mouth). Truthfully, he was a highly intelligent man with a lot of interesting information to share, but it was impossible for us to ever actually make a solid point before he interrupted. He was clearly incapable of learning anything new if he was so busy telling us what he'd already studied, himself. Furthermore, he was obstructing others' ability to learn anything new because we couldn't get on with our course.

After a couple days of trying to cordially engage his questions, we had to pull him aside and help him see that we wanted him to encounter something *new*. In order to do so, he had to put aside all that he already *knew*. If he could relax and listen more than speak, he might click into a different gear of learning. It is not uncommon that it takes participants two or three days to fall out of their "normal" and then actually be able to learn. What I mean by "normal" is that most adults in the business world have a "high idle." They are used to their mind running at a fast pace. They wake up and immediately start thinking about the day's tasks, what's going on at work that day, or in Carl's case, all the knowledge and ideas they have kicking around in their head. The volume is always up and the pace is always quick. The average adult mind does not have a lot of empty space. And that's not very conducive to learning. My friend, teacher and then business partner for over six years, Aaron, had the best metaphor for this phenomenon and the patience it requires when working with clients. He compares our job to trying to flick playing cards through the blade of an electric fan. If the fan is on high, every single card is just going to get flicked right back at us. But if we can help people un-plug, (i.e., stop thinking so fast and so loud about all the *stuff* we normally think about), the blades start to slow down and eventually, some cards can slip through the space in between. Many people I work with notice the same thing happens to them on vacation. They don't really begin to enjoy themselves until three to five days into the trip because their mind was still all sped up and thinking about work. To his credit, Carl did click into a different gear eventually. By the third and fourth days, the entire group had really moved into a different space. People were no longer irritated, impatient and intellectually combative. As we discussed the internal workings of the mind and the spacious potential that resided there, people became more reflective, intrigued and started asking questions and sharing new insights. There was space, and some cards could get through. They started learning.

On the morning of the fourth day, one of the participants that had been sitting next to Carl throughout the program raised his hand and said, "I have a question for you. What have you done to Carl? He feels like a different person. And I've never seen him be this quiet for this long. What's going on over there?" The man asking the question was being both playful but genuinely curious to know what was happening inside of Carl. I looked in Carl's direction and asked, "Well, would you care to share?" He looked around the room for a bit, inhaled and then gave us the most fascinating description of what he was experiencing. And in his story, underneath it you can hear the evidence of the principles we'd been discussing with them:

"You know, it's a funny thing. All my life, I've been an intellectual. I've studied and learned so much information. And I've prided myself on this knowledge. It's like I built this amazing library in my brain. And in this library, there are books on almost every topic. It's really quite impressive. You need a book on quantum mechanics? I've got it. You need a book on religions of the world? I've got it. Engineering? Math? History? Anything? You name it. And I know exactly which books sit on which shelves, and I've read them all a hundred times. I'm a master of all of them. But as I've been sitting here in this class the last couple of days, it's almost like someone lightly tapped me on the shoulder and whispered, 'You know, there's a door over there.' And I seem to have walked over and opened this door to discover that outside this library is an entire mansion. There are other rooms. And then there's a door from the mansion to the lawn outside and beyond. There's just so much more than this little library. What my mind already knows is so small in comparison to what I haven't explored yet, what I haven't thought yet. So I guess I'm just quietly walking around, exploring the new scenery. It's fascinating and it feels very big. So much bigger than where I'd been living before. I'm looking forward to going back to my work and my family more in this space of unknown."

Everyone in the room had sweetly surprised smiles come over their faces as they listened to him. You could sense the genuine humility of what Carl was experiencing, and everyone was both thrilled for him *and* for themselves. It was evident from observing the group in the first few days that Carl was someone people tolerated. His unconscious but constant interruptions were clearly something everyone got a taste of, not just my colleagues and me. From overhearing small side conversations during breaks and lunches, I gathered he was the guy that people rolled their eyes at in meetings, as he was often cutting people off and interested only in his own ideas. So to hear him take a step outside the library of his own impressive intellect was not only a breath of fresh air for Carl, but also for all of those who worked with him.

People beginning to listen and be less interested in the chatter of their normal thinking, regardless of how impressive and smart it may seem, is a common outcome of learning the three principles. While it may not seem obvious just reading it here on the page, the ripple effect of someone listening more from a space of what they *don't* know is a complete game changer in terms of relationships, productivity, the flow of meetings, innovation and design and even sales.

And then there was Dylan. Adorable Dylan. He was younger, probably late 20s/early 30s, thick Irish accent, with dark hair and light eyes. He was quite handsome. I remember thinking he was like a handsomer version of Jake Gyllenhaal. He *really* struggled for the first few days of the course, and he was not trying to hide it one bit. It was not intentional or obnoxious, but he just couldn't help himself. His leg shook up and down, he tapped his foot on the floor, or his hand on the table constantly. He even said to me, "Come on, Mara, you're killing me! This is just too slow and singularly focused for me. I'm the kind of guy that needs to be doing twenty different things at the same time not to get bored." He was being honest, and I understood his suffering. It was genuine. But I also knew that if he hung in there and got past the discomfort of the space in his mind, he'd eventually encounter some new thoughts. Because mechanically, that's how we all work. It's only when the whirring fan blade of our mind has an opportunity to slow down that something new can come in. That's why people consistently list places like taking a shower, while running, or being on vacation as where and when they get their best ideas. Not "at the office while I'm doing twenty different things."

Also on the morning of the fourth day, after Carl had described his exploration of the mansion and beyond, Dylan raised his hand and said, "I want to share something. I had a really fascinating experience this morning taking my two little kids to school." I hadn't even noticed Dylan yet that day. It was like he'd gone invisible, which was telling. His leg wasn't shaking. His foot wasn't tapping. His energy and presence were much quieter.

He continued, "I usually hate taking my kids to school, so I make my wife do it. She's much better at it. I have real young ones, a three and five year old, so walking them to school takes, like, seven hours because they want to stop every few feet to pick up a rock on the sidewalk or point something out to me. Their school is only a few blocks from our house, but it takes an eternity to walk there because I feel like I'm dragging them. It drives me nuts. But last night, my wife told me she had an early meeting at work, so she would need me to take the kids to school. I whined at first and was about to argue with her, and then I remembered this course and what we've been learning, and I thought, *Wait, it's all in your mind, right? You're only ever feeling your thinking, right? It's not the circumstance.* So I said, "OK, sure. I'll take the kids to school."

So the next morning, I walked the kids to school, and the craziest thing happened. I didn't even try to *change* my thinking. I didn't have to say, *Don't have annoyed thinking* as I was walking them down the street. I have no idea how I did it, but I just found myself walking them to school with *very little thought* in my head. And what I experienced was so cool. My kids, it turns out, are fascinating. They have these personalities and adorable senses of humor. And they're really smart if you just listen to the conversations they have with each other. It's brilliant! And I found myself wondering, *Were my kids always this fascinating!?* I mean, I love my children, but I never knew they were this interesting. And surprisingly, it didn't seem like it took that long to get to school. In fact, we got there faster than I wanted. I didn't want the experience to be over; I was enjoying it so much. And then I wondered, does it normally even take that long to walk them to school, or do I just think it does because I'm annoyed and impatient? So yeah, I had a really unique and amazing experience walking my kids to school this morning, and I felt as though I got to see them in a way I'd never seen before. I felt really grateful."

All the participants in the room were absorbed in Dylan's story, and you could see a couple of people had tears in their eyes, as it was such a touching, heartfelt story coming from a somewhat surprising source. I, myself, was extremely moved by Dylan's story and assumed it was over, but then he said after a long pause, "But wait, that's not even the best part! After I left my kids at school and turned around to walk back to the house, I suddenly had the realization, *I'm not bored!*" He paused for a few seconds and looked around the room with wide eyes and wonder on his face. "No, seriously. I was not bored. For the first time in years, I didn't feel bored or in a hurry to get to the next thing. I know you guys don't realize how huge that is for me, or maybe you do, ha ha ha, but seriously, I'm normally *always* bored. And there's this fear that if I'm not moving or doing something all the time that I'm just going to get swallowed up by boredom. But walking back to my house this morning I realized I wasn't bored. And *then* ..." At this point, Dylan's eyes got excited and he was leaning forward in his seat. "... I realized *life* isn't boring. *I'm* boring. I'm bored of my *self!* Or really, I'm bored of all my thinking. When my thinking quiets down, then suddenly I actually see life. And life is pretty fascinating. My kids are pretty fascinating. I suppose that's why they always say 'live in the moment.' Because the moment isn't boring. It's your *thinking* that gets boring! It's the only thing that can make you feel boredom. Really, you guys have no idea how huge this is for me, because I've been bored for so long. And I'm not bored anymore. I assumed it was something to do with the world outside of me, and it's not. It's great!" He glanced at me and grinned really wide and said, "So I guess this class isn't killing me after all."

There were several other profound and beautiful stories that came from the participants in that group. I learned so much from working with them. That group was one of the largest teams I'd worked with from a single business, and it was early on in my career when I still got nervous and doubtful at times. Their impatience and frustration made me doubt our course at moments. But we hung in there with them and kept pointing them back in the direction of the internally created nature of reality – and the fact that as our thinking becomes quieter, and less solid looking, it falls away in surprising ways. In a different state of mind, all of life looks different. Universally, all human beings stumble on that fact as their mind shifts into a different space. It's guaranteed. Working with that group really proved that to me because every last one of them had insights or "a-ha" moments by the end of the course.

What is amazing about talking about something as neutral as the principles of *mind, consciousness and thought* is that we never even got into personal applications, like "how to stop living in the arrogance of your own intellect" or "how to enjoy your children more," and so on. These are just natural applications that people make for themselves as they're learning. Learning about this understanding of the mind really leads to an *across the board* change in people. Because a person's state of mind precedes everything they do, whether it be parenting, playing golf or managing a team of engineers. When we learn something so fundamental about the mind, "all boats rise with the tide."

As you can imagine, we are typically hired by businesses to work with a team so that they get better at their jobs, not so that they necessarily become better at walking their kids to school. Much to people's surprise, after four days of talking about the internal principles of the mind, when we shift gears and talk about their business again, people find they've become *far* better thinkers about their business challenges without even knowing it. On the final half-day of that group's program, we talked solely about their business challenges. We discussed timelines, budgets and meeting structures. What was fascinating to observe is that 30 people in a completely different state of mind from where they started had a completely different kind of conversation. They were unbelievably present, clear and inspired. They listened to each other differently. Again, it is typical that people become better versions of themselves in clearer states of mind. They become better athletes, better parents, better coworkers and better engineers. Why? The obvious answer is because people who feel better, do better. But even more than that, the human mind is like a processor. It only has so much bandwidth, and as that bandwidth gets overcrowded with too much thinking about work, budgets, deadlines, insecurity, frustration and so forth, the processing power of the mind is greatly diminished. Taking a step back from the job, seeing that we aren't dealing with all the noise out there, but rather dealing with the noise that's generated in our mind, and being able to drop out of much of it and free up space allows for people to access a cleaner, clearer, more powerful version of their mind.

The "Carls" of the group were humble, curious and open. The "Dylans" were present and not impatiently distracted. They were inspired to have the conversation about their business, as opposed to dreading it. They completely redesigned their approach to one of their projects and determined that the way they'd been going about it before was inefficient. Many of them said they were looking forward to going back to work on Monday and that they hadn't felt that way in a very long time. One of them said, "I used to dread our Monday meetings, and now I think they're actually going to be beneficial, given what we've learned about our state of mind." They were also shocked at how much they were able to accomplish and how many lingering problems they were able to solve in only a half-day meeting (9 am to 12 pm). One woman gushed, "I feel like we got more done in the last few hours than we have in our meetings over the last year!"

It's comments like that, which I hear over and over again from clients and teams, that make me so inspired and curious: what might we actually be capable of if more people in more companies were operating from a state of mind that was that efficient and that enthusiastic? Oh, and not to mention, they get to go home and enjoy their children more, too.

In that aerospace company, we ended up working with dozens of teams and hundreds of their employees over several years. During the time period that the three principles were being shared in the company, according to their president, "Every single metric we measure improved: attrition went down, sick days went down, productivity went up, sales went up, client satisfaction skyrocketed. There wasn't one thing we measured that wasn't positively affected by our learning these principles."

Four

The Mediation

*"You can't solve a problem from the same
level of thinking that created it."*

– Albert Einstein

A round the same time early in my career, I was invited to
facilitate a mediation between an engineering team and
government auditors. I know, you're probably thinking what I
was thinking at that time: "Why would someone in my field be
invited to do a mediation?"

In a different part of that same multinational aerospace
company we'd worked with in England, this time in the north-
eastern USA, there was a program within the company that was
struggling to pass its government audit. Without getting into
the complex details of how the government regulates aerospace

companies, just know that much like restaurants in New York City must pass regular health inspections, the US government has an annual auditing process it conducts with all aerospace companies with which it has contracts to make sure everything is adhering to strict regulations. Under this particular contract between the government and the aerospace company, the program had failed to pass its audit four years in a row. If the program did not pass its audit this year, it would be permanently shut down and the aerospace company would lose millions of dollars, be heavily fined and a large number of jobs would be lost. All of the hours of work and the technology they had designed thus far would not be put into the final phase of product execution. All in all, it would be a crushing blow for the company, financially and morally.

When I received the call from John, the team leader for the program at the aerospace company, he said, "We're at our wits end. We've tried everything we know to do, and we can't get a passing grade. It seems to us that these government auditors just have it out for us. We don't know what else to do, and we're willing to try anything. It's my understanding from other people at our company who've worked with you and your associates that you have a way of teaching people how to ascend to states of more clarity, regardless of the circumstances. Well, from where we sit, it seems like we're trapped in the worst circumstances possible. And we definitely don't see a clear way out. So we need a miracle to transcend this one. If you could somehow help my guys see a new way forward, that would be amazing. We have a two-and-a-half-day meeting scheduled with the government auditors in two weeks in Boston. It's a final meeting to go through some slides about the progress of the program before the last audit. It's our last chance. Historically, the meetings with the auditors have been very contentious, because my guys are under so much pressure, and they're really on edge. And the government auditors just seem ruthless. It's almost like they want the program to fail. So we can't have another meeting like the others. We need something different to happen. That's why I thought it might be a good idea to call you guys. Could you possibly mediate the meeting? Help them talk to each other and work *something* out?"

My initial response was fear. It seemed like a complex problem, and I had never mediated anything before in my life. I told John that I wanted to talk it over with my boss (who had taught me so much and always managed to see things simply where others could not), and that I'd also like to do brief, 30-minute phone interviews with the five team members, as well as the two government auditors so that I could get a clear understanding of how everyone was seeing the situation. We didn't have much time, as the meeting was only a couple of weeks away. I talked to my boss first and expressed my concerns, and he said, "Mara, you've got this. It's simple. You know the one thing that they can't see right now. People can't solve problems or find resolutions in a bad state of mind. People can only find answers in a good state of mind. So as a mediator, all you're responsible for is making sure they a) have a good state of mind during the meeting so that they can find new solutions and b) know *how* to have a good state of mind, no matter what. That's where the principles come in. Teach them that and you're good to go."

I realized he was right. The Einstein quote "You can't solve a problem from the same level of thinking that created it" was exactly why they had reached out to us. Essentially, John had called our company because he knew they needed a new level of thinking to solve this problem. And we could help them do that. So, my colleague, Keith, and I agreed to interview all the attendees the following week and fly to Boston to mediate the final meeting between the government auditors and the aerospace engineering team.

What we uncovered in the phone interviews was *exactly* what my boss had suggested.

People *cannot* solve their problems in a bad state of mind, and holy cow, did these people have bad states of mind. On *both* sides of the equation. The aerospace team talked about the government auditors like they were the scum of the earth. They had so much anger, frustration and impatience when they described them. They called them things like "power hungry," "typical lazy government workers," and "out to destroy us." When I spoke to the auditors, they described the aerospace engineers as "extremely arrogant," "horrible listeners," and "childish." "They want to pass their audit, and believe me," one of them explained to me over the phone, "*we* want them to pass their audit so we can stop dealing with them, but they never listen to us so they never make the necessary changes. There are *laws* and regulations they have to follow, just like everyone else." More than anything, both sides were frustrated – unbelievably frustrated. One thing was unanimous: both sides were hungry for some new resolution. They just didn't know how to get it.

When we arrived in Boston to begin the meeting, what we had heard in our phone interviews was only more evident in person. The engineers and the auditors looked like two packs of young school boys on the playground, ready to fight. There was lots of huffing and puffing, eye rolling and mumbling under one's breath as they greeted one another and settled on opposite sides of the table from each other. My colleague and I kicked off the meeting and said we wanted to set some guidelines that would help the meeting proceed in a different fashion than usual. We obviously didn't have a ton of time to go into depth, as we knew they had a lot of slides they'd need to get through, as well, but we wanted to spend the first half of day one sharing an understanding of the mind that helps people to do a few things differently than they might normally do. Firstly, it allows them to *listen from a blank slate*. The only way that people can see something new in an otherwise contentious relationship is to recognize that one's own thinking jumps in and interrupts them, keeping them from seeing and hearing something fresh. And old, upset thinking will keep us hearing the same thing over and over again.

Secondly, in order to have helpful, productive ideas, people have to be in a good state of mind. You can't be annoyed and in a good state of mind at the same time. It's impossible. So if you want productive thought, look after your state of mind. How do you do that? Well, we will teach you these basic principles of *mind, consciousness and thought* that show you how your state of mind is an internally determined experience. As much as it *appears* to be the opposite – that externals, like people and circumstances – determine your state of mind, it's actually an illusion.

The only thing that can make you have a shift in state, or a shift in feeling, is a shift in your thinking. You are only and always living in the feeling of your thinking. And no one outside of you can do your thinking *to you.* If you want to correct a bad state of mind, just stop blaming it on something outside of yourself, and realize that if you don't breathe more life into a thought, it can't continue without you. As Sydney Banks, the man who originally articulated the principles, used to say, "The life of a thought is only as long as you think it."

After laying this foundation, we then spent the rest of the morning giving a basic introduction to the principles and helping connect the dots to how these principles give you the roadmap for accessing a blank mind to listen from and how to look after your own state of mind. We took questions and had a rich discussion to help them understand it as clearly as possible. With this group, it was incredibly valuable to illustrate how the human mind has effortless access to new, responsive, intelligent ideas when it is clear or relaxed. Whereas, when the mind is tense, stressed, frustrated and hopeless, it's *universally impossible* to get intelligent ideas. While it's sometimes hard for people to see this fact in business, because so many people assume a stressed state is a normal state to be in at work, it's easier to see it in sports. Look at golf. Anyone who plays golf knows that you play worse when you're tense. That's because the same principles apply. Clearer states of mind do *everything* better than agitated states of mind. Thus, it's no surprise that they hadn't been able to pass the audit four years in a row. It was like continuing to make a bad shot in golf and just getting more upset for the next (predictably bad) shot.

The second critical point for this group was to be able to stop blaming each other for their bad state of mind. No matter how clearly one states it, it's endlessly easy to miss how we are living in the feeling of our own thinking and that we are always capable of accessing new thinking in any moment. No one else can do your thinking to you. That's why some people handle certain situations better than others, because it's not coming from the situation. It's coming from how we relate to our thinking about it. My colleague used to say, "The engine light on your dashboard is a warning that something's not right under the hood of *your* car. Not the car next to you. Blaming others for your bad state of mind is like rolling down your window and yelling to the car next to you, 'Hey, buddy, I think there's something wrong with your car, 'cause my engine light just lit up." This wasn't an easy notion for these warring sides to consider, but overall, both the auditors and the engineers seemed engaged and curious. The general tone in the room improved significantly. I wasn't sure that the few short hours of discussion were enough to make a dramatic change in their approach, but it felt like an encouraging starting point.

After we'd finished our discussion on the principles, we broke for lunch and came back to begin reviewing their slides. As mediators, we said, "OK, we're going to help keep an eye on the quality of listening and the quality of feeling in the conversation. If we see people not listening, then we're going to stop you. And if we see people's state of mind (i.e., feeling) slipping down, then we are going to stop you. Sound good?" They all agreed. As mediators, we had permission to keep an eye on those two factors, given that we'd agreed in our discussion that morning that those were the necessary requirements to achieve a new resolution. The next couple hours were, well, tough, to say the least. We were literally having to interrupt them every couple minutes to address either their listening or their state of mind.

Here's a brief example of what it looked like: The lead engineer would put up a slide and begin going over information. One of the auditors would say he had a question and instantly, every engineer would start rolling their eyes, sighing and mumbling to one another, "Ughhhh, seriously?" or "Here we go again!" Then, if the auditor didn't get an answer to his question, the tone of his voice would escalate and before you knew it, he was yelling. This happened in various forms over and over again, and every time we'd have to stop them and say, "OK, if you're rolling your eyes and mumbling, then you're unable to actually listen from a blank slate. Eye-rolling is a sign that you're annoyed. And you're obviously in some old, annoyed thinking. So let that thought go. Clear your head. Listen as if it's your first time in this conversation."

I know this might sound like ridiculous hand-holding or the kind of instruction that would make grown adults go nuts. Honest to goodness, though, this was how firm and directive we had to be. Time was of the essence. There was no wiggle room to waste precious hours on them staying in the same crappy head space they'd already been in for years. And as for the auditors, I finally looked at the one large gentleman who tended to raise his voice to a yell within seconds of not getting an answer he wanted, and I said curiously, "Do you know that you're yelling?" I honestly meant it as a question, not a reprimand. I wanted to know if he realized he was yelling: if it was intentional or not. "What?" he yelled back. I repeated myself, "Do you know that you're yelling? Your voice … it's very loud." "Oh," he said after a moment, "am I yelling? I didn't realize." And then he chuckled a bit and sat back quietly in his chair. You could feel his sincerity. Once pointed out to him, he could see it, but prior to that, his volume was totally inaudible from within his own head. "Yes," I continued, "it's generally harder to listen to someone when you feel like they're yelling. I think you'll get answers more readily if you look after your volume and tone a bit." Again, I know this sounds like we were being like marriage counselors or something, but it was necessary to point these things out to this group. Otherwise, the meeting just slid into a ditch unbelievably fast. We were able to get away with it for two reasons: 1) We had rapport with them, and 2) the discussion of the principles that morning had given a framework or context. Everything we were saying to them was supported by fundamental truths about how the mind works. So it wasn't just touchy-feely stuff. There was sound logic behind it.

By the end of that first day, it had been slow going. We'd only gotten through a handful of slides, and the number of times we had to stop the group to reset their listening and state of mind was painful to count. We agreed to stop for the evening. The government auditors thanked us, sincerely, for a very interesting first day and left, and the engineering team hung out to talk with us before they went to dinner. "Well," the most cynical and eye-rolling-est one of the bunch said, "I think we're done for. I think we can all assume this isn't going anywhere. We're not going to have jobs a month from now. I mean, you saw how absurdly ridiculous those auditors are." One of the newer, younger guys on the team piped up and said, "I don't know, I think Mara and Keith have a point. When we don't immediately react negatively to them asking a question or posing a concern, it's much easier to listen to them neutrally. I noticed that it got easier for me to hear their point. For the first time, I could kind of hear where they were coming from." The eye-roller got red in the face and said, "You gotta be kidding me! You felt like they were better today? We barely got anywhere!" And at this point the team broke into an argument. My colleague Keith, who is a very tall, probably 6' 6", large-statured person stepped in and said, both loudly but without a hint of aggression, "If you keep letting your thinking go to the same place, you're going to get the same result as before. You're going to *have* to try something different."

Then we dispersed and let the engineers go to the hotel bar and drink off the steam, while Keith and I went to dinner on our own. We typically dine with our clients when conducting a program, but in this case it seemed better to let them go have drinks on their own. I woke up the next morning and kind of shrugged my shoulders to myself. I had no idea what to expect. I don't want to say I was doubtful, because I'd seen enough people change profoundly and quickly to know it was *possible*, but I will confess I had a sort of, *this should be interesting* attitude. What I encountered when I came into the meeting room that day was most certainly interesting. It was actually downright shocking. Immediately upon entering I could feel that the engineers, who were already there, seated and quietly sipping coffee, were in a different space. There was a softness, almost even like a limpness, to them. They were not geared up or serious looking. No one was on edge. Some of them seemed downright relaxed. I looked around the room in puzzlement as I prepared myself a cup of coffee. A wave of fear/humor washed over me as I thought, "These guys must be totally hung over. They must've just gotten smashed at the bar last night." I walked over to the one guy I had deemed the sweetest, I think his name was Samuel, and I whispered, "Hey, Samuel … psst… what's up with you guys? Is everyone totally hung over?" He chuckled. "Ha. No. Not totally, anyway. Maybe a bit." "But everyone seems so …?" I searched for words. "I know," he said. "We kind of had a eureka moment over Budweisers last night. We decided, heck, if we fail the audit and lose our jobs, then that's it. We lose our jobs. It's over. There's no point kicking and screaming and making the final moments a big mess. So we all decided to just give up. Surrender. Quit fightin'. We'll do what you said and listen like good boys. And we'll try to be in a good state of mind. There's no point doing anything else at this stage. So, here we are. Hands up. Ready to listen. We realized you're right. Gotta try something different." I smiled slowly. "OK. I like the approach," I said. "It's fresh."

The auditors joined us within a few minutes and we got the meeting going. Again, I apologize for the seeming hyperbole, but I promise it's not misused. What unfolded in the meeting that day was nothing shy of miraculous. With the aerospace engineers setting a completely different tone, the meeting almost instantly started progressing much quicker than the day prior. The auditors started out like their usual selves, but they quickly changed tune to match the others. My big yelling guy actually caught himself starting to yell, and he looked at me and winked.

He said, with a sly grin on his face, "Whoa there. I was almost about to yell, but I caught myself. Did you see me, Mara? I caught myself."

It was adorably endearing. The whole group had a light playfulness about them. They were jokingly correcting their own listening and tone, and the meeting just kept progressing faster and faster. And then, it actually started to feel, for a moment, that perhaps we were having almost some version of weird fun. Then the quieter auditor jumped in (he had been a man of *very* few words) and said something that literally made my jaw drop.

He said, "You know, there's something that we've been doing during inspections that just makes your lives harder. We don't actually *have* to do it. In fact, there's a few ways in which we can partner more with you when we come for inspections, and that'll just move things along quicker. I mean, we all want this program to be successful, right?"

In my head, I thought, "Did he seriously confess to doing something just to mess with them, and then offer a way to make their lives easier? This is brilliant. Absolutely brilliant."

From that moment forward, the spirit of the discussion continued to progress from mediating a battle between two opposing sides, to observing a collaborative effort amongst a group with a singular goal. Not only did we get through all of their slides, we finished early. No one could believe it.

In the end, the auditors explained to the engineers, "Look, we would love to pass you, but in truth we can't – yet. We legally just can't right now. There are a few too many things not up to regulation yet. But we are happy to help you get to a passing grade, and we'll give you as much of an extension as necessary until we can get you to a passing grade, together."

The youngest engineer sighed and revealed a quiet, relieved smile. "That would be great. We would welcome any help you can give us, and I'll open up the floor to you and offer up any information. I can be much more transparent with information than we've been in the past. I know it will help move things along, and I'm looking forward to working together."

As the auditors packed their things up to leave, the big yeller walked over to me and said, "You know, I wasn't expecting to enjoy this meeting, but it was actually fascinating. You guys do really interesting work. And thanks for pointing out that yelling thing. I think my wife is going to be really grateful." And he shook my hand.

When it was just the aerospace engineers left, I said, "So ... happy?" "Yes!" Samuel replied. "Happy enough," the eye-roller said. "We're still alive, right? Still in the game. That's what we needed. So thanks for your help."

When I was on the Amtrak heading back to New York City, I called my boss at the time and I said, "Holy shit! This stuff really works." He laughed, and I explained that I always knew without a doubt that with a single shift in thinking, all new things could become possible, but I'd never fully appreciated *how* quickly an awful dynamic that had developed over years around a seemingly complex issue could change literally overnight, and where there had previously seemed no solution, there was now a way forward. I felt like I'd just been in a great movie that had a surprising plot twist in the end. It had never looked so clear to me that all complexity and difficulty is driven by lack of clarity. In a different state of mind, people see a simpler way forward. What a gift to know it's within us. It's within all of us.

Five

The Champion

*"The best way to make your dreams
come true is to wake up."*

- Paul Valery

I am one of those people you can call a "seasoned business traveler." I have my travel toiletry bag that's permanently packed. I have the mental checklist down pat. I used to have a "friend" at the security checkpoint in the Seattle airport because I was there so often. At various points in my career, it's not been uncommon to travel to five different states/countries/ time zones in a single month. Only once have I missed a flight for a business trip, and it was the classic "my alarm never went off" because my iPhone up and died. Not like, ran out of batteries, but crapped out altogether.

It showed no signs of its doom; it just expired one night while I was sleeping, unfortunately on a night when I had to wake up at 5:30 am the next day to catch a flight from JFK to Sea-Tac. So I naturally woke up around 6:45 am with that feeling of "Uh oh, I am entirely too rested. I never feel this good before 5:30." I realized I'd overslept and there was no way I'd make my flight, but in my groggy, discombobulated haze it still seemed like a good idea to rush to the airport while simultaneously calling Delta and trying to get on the next flight.

Long story short, I went all the way to the airport for nothing, because the next available seat was on a flight the following morning. To add insult to injury, I had been auto-upgraded to business class on the original flight, but on this new one I was to take, I had a middle seat in coach. As I boarded the plane for the five-hour trip to Seattle the next day, I had my comfy neck pillow with me, all ready to just get in my seat and pass out. I was so *over* this trip already, and it had barely begun.

When I sat down, a gentleman was already seated next to the window.

A friendly-looking guy with a big smile. But as I sat down, I thought, "Uh-oh, he's friendly, like really friendly, and he'll want to make friends and chat for the next five hours. No, thank you."

Please don't mistake me for some kind of Scrooge. I love people. I wouldn't be in this line of work if I didn't. I simply needed a serious nap. I hadn't slept well the night before (terrified of repeating the whole not-waking-up/missing-the-plane thing kept me waking up every hour or so throughout the night). I thought if I immediately put my neck pillow on and closed my eyes, that would function as a "do not disturb" sign. But I literally couldn't get that chubby pillow around my neck fast enough before he said, "Hi, I'm Jason. What takes you to Seattle?"

"Oh, um, work," I said casually.

"Oh. What do you do?" he asked.

I know from experience that describing my job to people often leads to a long conversation, for a few reasons: a) No one has ever heard of what we do, so they have a lot of follow up questions. It's not like I say, Oh, I'm in sales. Or fashion. Or IT; b) People often think they've heard of something *like* what we do, so they have a lot to say about that other thing that they think is similar (*Oh, is it like The Secret?* Or *You know, I've recently gotten into mindfulness.* Or, *have you heard of Landmark?*); or c) Most commonly, people are either openly or secretly fascinated by the untapped potential of the mind, so when I say that we educate people in an understanding of how we use the mind and how we can use it more effectively, it's like offering a kid a piece of candy. They love it.

At this moment in time, due to my desire for a short conversation, I found myself simply saying, "I'm a consultant." In my personal opinion, saying "I'm a consultant" is a conversation ender. It's boring. No one really knows what it means because it can mean so many different things, and rarely do people ask because they figure it won't be that interesting. But not friendly Jason.

He said, "Oh, really? What kind of consulting?"

"Oh, well, we mostly work with businesses and a few other fields to show them how to have more clarity of mind, independent of the circumstances at hand."

I honestly didn't think I'd said it in any way that would sound that interesting, but he lit up like a Christmas tree.

"Really!" he said. "That's fascinating! That stuff really fascinates me because I used to be a professional athlete, so I totally get that you can have these crazy experiences of clarity and focus, no matter how high the stakes are. Wait, so you talk to business people about this?"

I realized at this point that he and I were going to be having an in-depth conversation whether I wanted to or not. And the truth is, I can't help myself. I like my work and people too much, so I was starting to want to have the conversation. Especially given how quickly he seemed to pick up on what we do and how he had his own personal experience of it as an athlete. I was intrigued.

Before I knew it (I think we were taxiing down the runway to prepare for takeoff), Jason was in tears, more or less sharing his life story with me. I'm going to paraphrase, because we pretty much talked the entire five-hour flight. He asked how we teach business people about unconditional clarity of mind and I said, "Well, essentially we talk with them about the fundamental principles that underlie the human experience. *Mind (which is the intelligence or the energy of all things), consciousness (which is what makes us aware, and allows us to feel) and thought (which is the content we have come into our mind which creates a picture of the world).* They are like the elements that combine to create our experience moment to moment, but they're so seamless and invisible that it looks like it's the outside world determining our experience. So we have the illusory sensation of being 'reactors' to our perceptual experience, rather than the 'creators' of it. When people begin to look inside and consider that it's all an inside job, it makes them more reflective and less reactive, and their relationship to their thinking becomes lighter and softer. People hold on to their thinking less tightly. So their thinking begins to flow more effortlessly. Before you know it, people start experiencing states of what you might describe as ease or flow, presence or clarity in all kinds of moments where it previously had seemed out of their grasp."

His eyes started to well up with tears, and he said, "I know exactly what you're describing, because I had that exact feeling of flow, of complete internal clarity every time I stepped foot on the tennis court, but I've never been able to figure out how to get it anywhere else in my life. And I've always struggled with that. And now my life is, well, it pretty much sucks. I have a job I hate, working for a big corporation and my wife – ughhhhh. I think my wife wants to leave me. Or I want to leave my wife. I'm not sure. But I know we're not happy. And I don't really play much anymore. I had one bad tournament several years ago, and I just decided that was it. My time was over. I wasn't going to compete anymore. And it's been years since I've had that feeling I used to have on the court all the time. It was spiritual, that feeling. It was the one place where everything felt *just right*."

He paused for a long while and just cried, silently, looking toward the window from time to time.

One Thought Changes Everything

"So if I hear you, you're saying that people can have that feeling anywhere?" "Yes," I said. "They can. Because it's not the circumstances. It's something that's happening from within. I mean, think about it. Where do you think it came from when you played tennis? The court? The ball? Did something in the air seep into your lungs and create that experience inside of you?"

He sat there, pondering for a bit. I was genuinely surprised when he came back to me with, "Well, yeah, it always seemed like there was something special in the court. Like, once my feet made contact with the court. So yeah, it seemed like that's where it came from: the court."

I wanted to laugh because it seemed so silly, but I realized that superstition is so common and so easy to get caught up in in the sports world. *It's my lucky socks. It's the home field advantage. It's my favorite ball. Don't step on the lines of the court.* What's so easy to miss about superstitions, or all external things, is that they just trigger a mental shift. But it's still coming from the mind. All of life that we experience originates in the mind. If it was in the *thing* (the socks, the court, the whatever), then it would work the same for everyone, every single time. And obviously, it doesn't.

It's the same reason money can't make you happy. If it was in the money itself, all rich people would be happy. And we know that's not the case. Essentially, what makes people happy is where they allow their mind to relax. Where their thinking goes quiet. And when people's thinking goes quiet, that greater impersonal intelligence, or that bigger energy we describe as *mind,* has the space to play more. That's why when top tier athletes talk about a great game, they describe it as Jason did: spiritual. Meaning, "beyond me." You hear musicians or dancers refer to this as well: "during the concert, I let the music play itself," suggesting that if we get our thinking out of the way, a natural flow of intelligence takes the stage. And it's in those moments that people feel in sync with life, rather than in battle with it.

Jason and I talked for hours about how ever since he quit competing, his life had gone downhill. He'd taken a serious job, making good money to satisfy his wife and parents, who'd spent lots of money on his Ivy League education, when in truth, all he wanted to do was go back to playing tennis, maybe set up a clinic or camp for high school kids, and travel. Italy. He loooooved Italy and he had what he thought of as a ridiculous dream to somehow combine his love of tennis with his love of Italy. Maybe some kind of touring tennis camp where he could introduce kids to the pleasures of Italian art, food and culture, while also teaching them to play tennis.

Anyway, it all sounded so stupid, he thought.

I assured him that none of it sounded stupid to me and that I knew for a fact that if he could find the same clarity and quiet he found on the court in his other areas of life, he'd experience the same spiritual feeling that everything was just *right*. There was absolutely nothing in his way, other than how he'd started using his thinking against himself in those areas and that if he spent some time learning about the real "operating system" of the mind, he could see how to undo that. In fact, I felt my colleague at the time, a fellow named Dicken, was a perfect match for him. I suggested he book a program with Dicken and gave him the contact info.

"Oh, I'm going to," Jason said. "I know you probably don't believe me, but I'm literally going to call and book it right after we land. I can already tell this is changing my life, just from our conversation."

As we landed, he gave me a big hug and said, "You know, I wasn't even supposed to be on this flight. I missed my flight last night, so they put me on this one."

"Ha! Really?" I said. "I wasn't supposed to be on this flight, either! I missed my flight yesterday morning, and this was the earliest I could get out. I was all annoyed, too, because I was supposed to be in business class on the other flight, and on this one I was stuck in a middle seat in coach … next to you!" I gave him a sweet, joking smile.

"Well, I know some people don't believe in that stuff," he said, "but I definitely think it was no accident we both missed different planes and ended up here together on this one. I'm so glad I didn't make that other plane."

"Me, too."

Jason lived not too far from me, so a few months later he reached out and suggested we get lunch. He wanted to thank me, as he'd gone through the program with Dicken and, as promised, it had been life changing. He said, "Not a day goes by that I don't feel grateful for what I've learned. It's changed everything."

Over the next year, Jason and I got together for lunch a few times, and I watched as he completely transformed his life. He started playing tennis competitively again and actually ended up making quite the career comeback. He is currently the no. 1 ranked player in his age group in the world.

He said to me over lunch once, "I thought I was good before, but now I'm really good.

Like *really* good. I'm beating these young 20-somethings and I'm 40! They hate me!"

"What do you think has changed?" I asked.

"Well, it's actually pretty crazy. I don't know that anyone else will understand this but you. I used to think that playing well was about clearing your head and focusing on only the positive thoughts that come in. So I would try to push negative thoughts aside. But even that created some work. Some distraction. Some noise in the system. Since learning about the principles, I've realized that all thought is just a temporary form in your mind. Negative or positive. It's all just an energy taking a form and then dissolving again. If you don't pay attention to any of it, you kind of just start to fall into this wide open space. It's raw energy.

"And then – this is the part that sounds crazy – you almost start playing beyond the boundaries of time. You kind of move and respond, knowing what's going to happen before it's happened. Like my legs just start going in a direction and then it turns out that's exactly where I was supposed to be to get the ball. That's why I can beat 20 year-olds. They're in much better shape than I am, for sure. But my mind is so free that it's almost like I'm playing psychic. Ha! I know that must sound crazy, but it's really awesome."

To me, it didn't sound crazy at all. It actually reminded me of my experience in Buenos Aires and how when my thinking had gone so quiet, I felt I had a kind of super knowing.

"I definitely know what you mean," I said.

He'd also left his job working at the company he loathed and was now working as a tennis pro and as a director at two different clubs and was launching his first Italian tennis camp for kids that summer. The man was literally living out his dream: a dream that he had previously deemed ridiculous and impossible.

I asked how things were with his wife, and he said things were so-so. She was a little flipped out about him leaving a secure job and pursuing all his dreams, so he wasn't totally sure how things were going to pan out. But he didn't seem sad or lost. It was just the final kink he was still working out.

He and I haven't had lunch in a while; in fact, it's been a few years since I've talked to him. But I know from good ol' Facebook that he eventually divorced his wife and has now been dating a woman for quite some time who seems madly in love with him. He looks incredibly happy. Last time I checked, he's still the no. 1 ranked tennis player in the world in his age group.

Six

Ice Man

*"Every man takes the limits of his own field
of vision for the limits of the world."*

- Arthur Schopenhauer

A few years ago, my former partner, Aaron, and I worked with a United States marine, Brian, nicknamed "Ice Man," as part of a documentary film about the ripple effects of IEDs (improvised explosive devices) and the pervasiveness of PTSD among returning veterans. A filmmaker named Dani reached out to me via email one day out of the blue. She and I had gone to the same high school but were a couple of years apart so did not know one another well. It had been suggested that she reach out to me via a friend of mine whose husband was a marine. She had been poking around her networks looking for subjects for her film, which focused on the ripple effect of a single IED. The intended project is to create a "feature-length documentary and multi-media outreach project that explores the invisible wounds of war and the stigmas surrounding behavioral health in the military through combat veterans' most intimate relationships." Dani was curious about what we did, as she'd heard we had worked with wounded veterans in the past. She was hoping to include not just the trauma and tragedy of her subjects' stories, but also a vision for resilience, hope and a real solution to PTSD. She was hoping we would consider working with one of the men as part of her film to demonstrate a treatment that might actually *work*. I was intrigued and excited about the potential of the project to shed light on the possibility for people to find freedom of mind, even after traumatic experiences like war. We had worked with a few wounded veterans in the past with huge success, but it had never been filmed, and thus could not be shared on a broader scale. After several emails and meetings, we arranged to film a four-day program of Aaron and me working with Brian, who was a Master Sergeant Marine with over 20 years of service. His platoon's role in Iraq had been the subject of an HBO documentary. He is also now a speaker on post-combat stress issues. Over the four days, we would dialogue with Brian about the principles underlying the mind to see a) if it provided him any insight into his own life and leadership as a marine, both in terms of dealing with his past experiences and current leadership responsibilities in the military, and b) if he felt the three principles training offered a new solution for dealing with post-combat stress and trauma issues.

It was quickly evident how Brian had earned the nickname Ice Man. He had a stern, composed face. It wasn't harsh or terrifying, more just expressionless. He showed little emotion. Before we began the four-day program, we all had dinner together – Brian, the film crew, Aaron and myself – as a way to get to know each other a bit before we dove into the project. I noticed that even as we sat around the dinner table sharing friendly stories about our lives, he would smile and laugh when appropriate, and yet you didn't feel any sense of joy or actual laughter. What you *did* feel was a highly refined intelligence and a Herculean sense of control. He was watching everything. Absolutely *nothing* gets past this guy. I personally found him a mixture of intriguing and unsettling to be around. And I also felt that he knew that and liked it that way.

We began our program with Brian, laying out the three principles of *mind, consciousness and thought*, as an explanation of how all human experience comes from within a person. We further discussed the ability for all people to see the illusory and temporary nature of thought, such that they could let go of stressful feelings or bad memories that were carried through time via repetitive thinking. We explained that the veterans we, and other people in our field, had worked with that suffered from trauma found it incredibly freeing to learn about the special effects tricks that "thought storms" can play on us. Knowing that a flashback is just an incredibly powerful illusion caused by thought, made to feel real by consciousness, was comforting to them. And that if left alone, all thoughts will pass. Even really compelling or repetitive ones. It was incredibly hopeful for traumatized soldiers to learn that they were not broken. Nothing is wrong with them. They're falling for the same tricks of the mind as everyone else.

Brian nodded a lot. He felt that it made a lot of sense. He asked pointed questions here and there. Generally, he felt that as a Marine, it was already obvious that everything was in your mind. He agreed with us, but with politeness and a straight face, he said he didn't really get what the big deal was all about. It didn't seem that profound or new for someone like him. This is not an uncommon reaction at first. Some people really fight the notion that life is an inside-out game, as they're wedded to the perception that they are at the mercy of life's circumstances. But other people, like Brian, already agree that human experience is very much influenced by the mind and that we have a huge capacity to exercise "mind over matter." I don't imagine one would last long as a Marine if they *didn't* see this! It is also true that in many ways, the fact that thought creates our experience of life is a pretty simple and obvious fact. Everyone knows somebody (an in-law, a coworker, a friend) who creates an overly negative view of the world and wholly believes it's the world, whereas to those of us on the outside, it is clear it's how they think about life.

The interesting thing about Brian is that he gave off the impression that he already "knew" everything that we were talking about, yet he didn't feel content. Or at ease. He didn't seem like someone who was at peace with his understanding of life. He seemed tight, restrained and burdened. And there was obviously a reason he was sitting there with us. He wouldn't have agreed to do the program if he wasn't curious. There was something more that this man was hungry to understand, but he didn't know what. Because similarly to Carl, he already *knew it all.* Yet, as is so often the case, the longer we pointed in the direction of the fact that underneath the heaviness, the solidness and the hard limits of the thinking we live in day in and day out, there is a deeper, impersonal intelligence: an innate capacity to see beyond the four lines we've drawn around our experience of life. Just beyond our ideas lies a deeper feeling of the energy of life. The limitless capacity to experience a moment without the filtering of all our personal thinking about it. As we continued to point in that direction, Brian became more reflective, softer and more curious.

During the midday break on our third day, Brian opted to go for a walk around Manhattan by himself. When he came back in the afternoon, it was clear that something had happened and Brian had clicked! Much to our surprise, he felt completely different when he walked in for that session. He was very excited (and it actually showed on his face) to share something with us. He explained that for some strange reason, he'd wandered over to Times Square. He found it odd that that's where he went on his walk, because typically a place like Times Square would have driven him nuts, being around all those stupid tourists. He explained that he normally found average, everyday people to be annoying. Crowds of tourists were the last thing he'd want to be around. Yet today, as he was walking through all these mobs of people, for the first time he found himself seeing the world without all of his usual critical, militant, rigid thinking. His constant assessing and analyzing people and his surroundings had fallen away. "Normal Brian" went quiet. He found himself in an elevated state where he felt incredible clarity, love and hope for humanity that he had never experienced. As he described this experience of falling out of his normal chatter and into this deeper feeling, his eyes started to well up. And there before us, "Ice Man" began to melt. In his place sat this incredibly warm and feeling-full person. As tears streamed down his cheeks he said, "I've never felt that kind of connection to people before. It was such a deep feeling of love." Aaron and I sat silently and let him soak in this new discovery. It turns out, there was more to feel in life than Brian had ever known.

What was so fascinating to watch as Brian described his new insights he'd had over lunch, was that once he had a *feeling* of the principles behind life, he was suddenly "all in." He could see that there was a deeper potential underlying the smallness of our thoughts. He had glimpsed and felt something deeper than his intellect. He suddenly realized how there really *was* something profoundly different on offer when you learned about the full, true nature of the mind. Now his mind was unleashed and overflowing with new ideas about how a realization of these principles was precisely what the military needed. He said that an understanding of the three principles should be a part of pre-deployment training, and he felt it was even *more* important that military personnel be exposed to this learning *before* they went overseas. He was completely convinced that pre-deployment training in the principles would teach them how to be resilient in the face of the two most challenging aspects of being away from home: combat and boredom. As he described it, being in the military vacillates between being extremely exciting and exceedingly boring. When you're in the thick of the excitement, it's often easier to be clear (the "gun-to-your-head" phenomenon). There's a way in which your thinking clears out of the way automatically when there are bullets flying through the air. But then things can get very boring. You can spend weeks on end in the desert without much to do. *That* is when people's thoughts begin to creep up on them and start to become dysfunctional. They start replaying things over and over in their mind, and lots of people start to drive themselves crazy doing this. Looping frightened, angry or confused thinking was often the bigger cause of psychological trauma. Brian could see that if they understood the nature of thought, they would be immune to this prevalent, needless suffering.

Then, of course, even more importantly, the three principles understanding arms people with a uniquely simple and empowering understanding of trauma. Resilience and real, lasting recovery come from the knowledge of *how thought works*. No matter what happens to us, if we can let the thought storms that our memory throws at us ride like dark clouds over the land of our experience, we don't have to go insane thinking the sun of well-being has been destroyed. It can only ever temporarily be covered. PTSD does not have to be a death sentence. With the right understanding of the mind, anyone can heal. Brian was so excited that he had found what he felt was the missing piece in military training. We could not believe how inspired he was. He wouldn't stop talking about all the different ideas of how we could start to roll out the training: which group, at which training base. The Ice Man was on fire.

Given his insights and the incredible enthusiasm that followed, I was disappointed that after a couple weeks we lost contact with Brian. He got busy with his duties as Master Sergeant again, and I eventually got the disappointing feeling that he'd forgotten us. However, just as I was beginning to give up hope, I was contacted again by Dani, just a week ago as I'm writing this paragraph, who said that Brian had not forgotten us at all. That actually, he still talked about the program often and his belief in its effectiveness was as strong as ever. Even better news, is that Brian's term as Master Sergeant Marine is up. He is retiring from the Marines and planning to consult on best practices and veterans' affairs, especially focused on solving the PTSD and suicide epidemic. Turns out that he is very interested in rekindling the conversations to determine how we can bring this understanding to better prepare and help to heal the suffering people who serve our country. I'm pleasantly surprised and delighted to end this chapter with a *to be continued ...*

Seven

THE BASEMENT DWELLER

*"Everyone is doing the best they can, given
the thinking that looks real to them."*

- SYDNEY BANKS

One of the best parts of my job is constantly being re-minded I'm wrong. Like all human beings, I have think-ing run through my head all the time, and I don't necessarily see it is just my own made-up thinking. It feels *right*. Like my ideas about people. When I was new to this work, I didn't see it at the time, but I would think up ideas about the people in our courses.

Like, for example, "Oh, that woman is going to really get a lot out of this course. She seems very open and curious." Or, "That guy will be a tough cookie. He seems really closed and resistant." Then, to my shock, as the course would go on I'd discover that I had it all wrong. The "tough cookie" would end up being really engaged, and the "open and curious" woman would end up being a disruptively resistant know-it-all. I finally caught on to the fact that I'm often wrong in what I make up about people, and the truth is, *I don't know what's going to happen*. People are often surprising. Like Joe.

Joe was part of a large IT company we were working with in the Washington, D.C., area. We had been hired to roll out a program across several departments called "Leading From Within." We had designed the program to address the issue that the general culture of the company had become one of victimhood, blaming and lack of leadership. Many people in the company, even at the leadership level, complained about the "company culture" as if it was somehow a separate entity that had nothing to do with them. There was a lot of focus on what was wrong, but not much initiative being taken to make things better. We were brought in to help illuminate the fact that leadership is a state of mind, that it comes from within people, and that it comes from all people at all levels of the organization. Joe was a participant in one of the first groups of 20 or so that we worked with. As I said, I'm not proud of it, but I'll admit that I kind of wrote Joe off within the first few hours of the course. He appeared to be generally "checked out." Not just in our course, but in life. He looked bored, or just resigned. Again, I had no basis for this assessment other than I made it up based on his appearance and body language. He didn't seem alert or interested, so I guessed that there wasn't much going on upstairs. I assumed either he wasn't really interested in the course, or he was busy thinking about other stuff.

Over the next couple of days, we introduced the idea that all of life as we experience it is coming from the interplay of thought and consciousness. So we aren't living in a feeling of the world outside of us, but rather we are living in the feeling of our thinking. And the great news is, if we don't like the feeling we're living in, all we need to realize is that it's coming from thought. If we don't believe in it, invest in it or do something else to keep it alive and kicking, all thought will naturally fade. Mind, that intelligence that's running our system, will naturally bring in new thinking when there's space for it. Therefore, we are never stuck "in life." We only ever get stuck in old, unhelpful ways of thinking. I recall one participant in a course said playfully, "Aw, man! You're taking away one of my favorite phrases: 'I'm stuck between a rock and a hard place.' Now I'm realizing you can only ever be stuck between a thought and a thought, and thought is not solid. Or even real! So there's no such thing as stuck. I guess I'm going to have to find a new favorite saying."

We always check in with the group and ask people to share examples they can see in their own life that illustrate how experience comes from thought or how when thought changes, we suddenly don't feel stuck anymore. On the second day, we were going around the room and trying to hear from some of the quieter people. My colleague called on Joe and asked if he'd seen any examples of these principles at play in his own life. I wasn't expecting him to say much, as I had assumed he wasn't taking much in. But then he said, "I realized I don't have to live in the basement anymore." He said this very matter-of-factly, but with a surprising amount of feeling and energy behind it. It was almost like a declaration. It completely caught me off guard. He continued to explain: "Every night when I come home, I walk in the house and go straight to the basement. I give my wife a quick kiss on the cheek. I say 'hi' to my daughter, who is usually playing in her room or watching TV in the living room. I walk right past them and go downstairs to the basement, where I usually put SportsCenter on the TV and set up my laptop to keep doing work. I do this not because I don't want to be with them, but because I figure they don't want to be around me. I'm always stressing about work, and I've got a million things to do, so I figure it's just better for everybody if I'm in the basement because I don't imagine I'm very fun to be around.

"I'm generally pretty tense and stressed. I've got a lot on my mind all the time. Even if there aren't any urgently important issues at work, I'll still just keep emailing because my mind is always whirring, and I feel like if I can just get to the end of my to-do list, it'll stop. But I'm beginning to realize that it's my mind that needs to stop. All that thinking I'm playing over and over and over, I just need to turn it off. And for the first time in a really long time, I walked in the house last night, and I started walking toward the basement door, and then I stopped myself. And I thought, 'I don't want to go in the basement anymore. I'm sick of being in the basement all the time.' So I didn't. And at first, I didn't know what to do with myself. I could feel my mind wanted to just keep thinking about work, but I decided to try what we've been learning about and just let it pass through my mind. It didn't have to be a compelling reality. It could just be thought clouds that come and then go.

"I looked around the kitchen and living room and waited for a new idea to come to me. And I saw my daughter sitting on the couch watching a kids' movie. Some Disney or Pixar something or other. So I went and sat down next to her. You know, it's funny." His face kind of lit up as he said this: "I don't know if you've ever watched a kids' movie, but they're pretty funny. I found myself cracking up a few times. I never thought I could enjoy watching a kids' program so much. But I found myself just having a really nice time. And my daughter cuddled up next to me. I didn't have a lot on my mind. I just felt very content on the couch with her. And I noticed that my wife kept saying it was time for my daughter to get ready for bed, but I didn't want her to go. I didn't want it to end. So I convinced my wife to let her stay up a little later than usual with me. My wife pretended to look upset so that my daughter wouldn't get the idea that it was OK to stay up late, but I could see that under the feigned upset, she was really happy to see me spending time with our daughter. Overall, I found I had a really nice night. It occurred to me that I could feel that way a lot more of the time. And then I could enjoy some of the other floors in my house."

A few moments went by as Joe just went quiet after sharing about his evening. I could sense that he wasn't done yet. There was something more he wanted to say. Everyone could feel it, so we waited in silence a few moments longer. He finally looked up and said, "And I know for certain that I'm not going to hit my daughter anymore." The silence in the room became even more silent. I felt goosebumps wash over me. "I don't know why I know," he said. "But I know that I know. It won't happen again. I'm certain. Because something has shifted in me. I realized that I don't need to let my thinking build up so much. And if I don't do that, I won't be tense and stressed all the time. So I won't hit her. I just know I won't. It's almost like that part of me went away last night. I can't relate to the person who used to do that." He said it with complete confidence, clarity and openness, sitting in a room full of his colleagues.

I was overwhelmed by so many different emotions after listening to Joe that day.

It humbled me to see how wrong I had been about him. He wasn't checked out. He was very much *there*. He may have been buried under a lot of stressed-out thinking, but just underneath that was a human being who just wanted to feel better and get out of the basement more often.

And when he did, it was like a light switched on inside of him. In fact, the longer I've worked with people, I've come to realize that at the most basic level we all want the same thing: to feel OK in life. We are doing the best we can with what we understand of life to just be OK. Not a "ho-hum" kind of OK, but a deep, profound knowing that we are OK. That nothing is wrong with us. That we are a good person.

And we all come up with different ways of coping when we don't feel OK. Some of us drink. Some of us hit our kids. Some of us go running. Some of us gamble online. Some of us meditate. I've worked with a lot of different human beings, from the very high achieving, to those hanging on by a thread, and everyone on some level is just trying to feel OK. Joe had discovered that if he let his thinking pass through him like clouds, he would find just that: a feeling of OK-ness.

The other feeling I had while listening to him was, yet again, that sense of awe that an understanding of the principles behind our experience took care of whatever people needed help with. It's the quintessential cure for what ails you. Just as my dad's program wasn't designed to show him how to be a better dad, our program with Joe wasn't designed to help him stop hitting his daughter. Yet that was something Joe was struggling with in his life, and learning about how his mind works addressed the issue for him. If you step back enough, you begin to see that every single aspect of life begins with the mind. So if you change your understanding of the mind, you can change anything in your life. The simplicity and the hope in that never ceases to amaze me.

Finally, I was struck by *how much* someone can change when they have a shift in their understanding of the mind. Layers of thought that were rock solid seem to fall away, and when they do, people often look and feel lighter and say things like, "Nothing has changed, but everything looks different." Or, "I feel like I've come home to a feeling I had as a kid but lost many years ago." Or, as Joe said, "I *know* things are going to be different now." Many people in my field refer to this as a "shift in consciousness." From a different level of consciousness or a different level of understanding, life looks completely different. But if you're like me, that degree of change in that short amount of time kind of sounds unbelievable. When I re-read the chapters I've written, I imagine there are more than a few readers thinking, "Seriously!? So Joe, here, just learned that thoughts were like clouds and now he's a changed man?" Honestly, it's somewhat unbelievable to me, too, and I witness it with my own eyes every day. I sometimes think of it like the black box on airplanes. Whenever there is a plane that crashes, the first thing investigators look for is the black box, or flight data recorder, so that they can know exactly what happened that led to the plane crash. Sometimes, planes go down in deep oceans and the black box is never recovered, so we never really know what happened. Sorry for the morbid comparison, but sometimes I feel like people want to find the "black box" that explains exactly how a person had a shift in consciousness. I can't tell you exactly how anyone has a shift in consciousness because it's an individual experience that happens inside someone. But I can tell you some of the consistent factors that seem to be at play, both when I've had my own personal shifts, and when I've witnessed them in others. As I've said, we share the same three principles of *mind, consciousness* and *thought* with every individual and team we work with. As I'm sure you could gather in reading chapter 3, the definition of those principles does not take a long time to convey, nor are the definitions of those words really what impacts people and causes deep insight. A real insight or shift in consciousness seems to occur when people are able to pull the car over, put it in park and shut the engine off for a while. Most people's minds are running at pretty high speed day in, day out. There's not a lot of room for reflection in a state of constant mental activity. Our courses usually last three to four days in a row. During that time, we don't keep people's minds busy with handouts, PowerPoint slides and exercises. We find that just sitting and discussing these principles and asking people to take a step back from the usual way of thinking and reflect, or get curious, opens people's minds in a way that is very new and often very enlightening. This process can be quite uncomfortable for some people at first (remember Carl and Dylan?). Ultimately, though, it feels incredibly restorative, and it is the birthplace for insight. New thought can only come when you're temporarily not absorbed in your old habitual thoughts. As Joe's mind quieted down during our course, he had the new thought that he didn't *have* to go to the basement. He didn't *have* to pay attention to his constantly whirring thoughts about work, and in the different feeling state those realizations allowed him, he saw that it was never necessary to hit his young daughter. The amazing thing about the mind, as you start to consider that these basic forces are always at play, is that from *nothing* comes *something*. You don't see something, and then suddenly you do. The mind is constantly generating new thoughts. But in order to get something new, you sometimes have to go to *nothing* first. Thus, pulling the car over and shutting off is a critical catalyst for insight and change.

The second thing that I would say is consistent with people having major insights is that once the principles have been laid out on the table, people can experiment with them in their own life. You can test principles, and if they're true, they hold water. Because these principles are true, most people inevitably have an "a-ha moment" where they realize something that had seemed external to them was really coming from thought all along. When people are invited to consider that all human experience is coming from thought and that thought comes and goes – it does not last long unless you give it a lot of attention and importance – they can begin to play with their experience. Playing with the human experience, rather than taking it as a given, can be a fun and, at times, shocking experience.

I'll share an example of one of my biggest insights that came to me as I was playing with my experience a bit and happened to have a moment of space in my mind at the time. During my first couple of weeks as an intern at Pransky and Associates, I sat in with many different types of clients, both individuals and groups. I felt I "got" the principles relatively quickly. It made logical sense to me, because I could see so clearly that different people had different perceptions of the same situation, so of course our experience came from thought, not the outside world.

BUT! There was one area of my life where I couldn't see how my experience came from thought; and that area was my relationship with my dad. Interestingly, even though I felt my father changed significantly after his experience of learning about these principles, I still held fast to the notion that he *made* me feel bad. Albeit less often than before he'd been out to Pransky and Associates, but he still made me feel bad when he was tense, angry or critical. The bad feeling I had around my father at times looked to me like it came from him 100 percent, not from my thinking. My story went something like this: "Well, I'm generally feeling fine in life, but then when my dad shows up and he's in a bad mood, I immediately feel bad, so it must be him that did that to me, right?" Furthermore, I had supporting evidence to back my story because I knew many other people who also felt bad when they were around my dad in one of his moods. So HA!! It had to be true! I wrestled with this one quite a bit in my mind. I pleaded with one of my colleagues, "But aren't there *some* people in life that really can make you feel bad?" His response was, "I know it can seem like it. Especially with the people we are closest to, because it's hard for us to see our thinking with those people. But no, it's not possible. No one can step inside your mind and *make* you feel something. Only your thinking can do that. It'd be like hitting yourself over the head with a hammer but blaming the person standing across from you. Once you see you're holding the hammer, you can put it down." Frankly, I found this answer mildly annoying because it clashed with my story. I wrestled with it in my head for a few more hours, and finally I thought, "Screw it! This is giving me a headache. I guess I just don't see it in this area." So I dropped it. I legitimately let it go from my mind. I proceeded to go about my evening, not thinking about it.

A couple of hours later, as I was cooking dinner, I recall checking on my rice to see if it was ready. There was nothing in particular on my mind. I was just spacing out, waiting for my rice to cook. All of a sudden, out of the blue I had a brand new thought come into my mind. I had an image of my father's car pulling up the driveway at my childhood house and me looking out the window and getting tense. I watched this little movie play out in my mind and I suddenly realized, "Oh my god. I would make myself feel bad before he even stepped foot in the house! He wasn't doing it. He couldn't be doing it! He wasn't even there yet." And suddenly I saw one domino drop and hit another, which hit another and another, and I saw that I *thought* in a tense way about my father my entire life, *even when he wasn't around.* I was overwhelmed by such a strong feeling of "Holy shit, it's true! It's been happening in my mind all along." I didn't know whether to laugh or cry. It seemed so hysterically simple, and yet OH MY GOD, I'd spent so many years of my life feeling victimized by his moods. In an instant, so many things I'd heard in my life before, but dismissed, now made sense. My close childhood friend used to say to me when I would be upset about him, "Why don't you just ignore him?" I always thought she just didn't get it. If he was her father, she'd understand why that wasn't an option. But in that moment, sitting in my kitchen staring at rice at 23 years old, I realized she was right. It was up to me how I felt around my father. It always had been. In that moment I felt weightless, and I had seen the truth of the principles on a far deeper level. I'd had my first major insight that made my entire world look different. And you notice that I didn't *do* anything to make it happen. I was just curious to apply these principles to my own life, and then in a moment where my mind was in neutral, there was space for something new to come in. And that new thought has made all the difference in the world. Just like Joe's realization that he didn't have to live in the basement did for him.

Eight

HITLER'S PROTÉGÉ

"The secret of genius is to carry the spirit of the child into old age."

- ALDOUS HUXLEY

I don't know if you've noticed yet, but I'm in love with my job. I get to meet some of the most fascinating people, from such a wide variety of backgrounds, and hang out with them, talk with them about the mind, learn from them and watch them have profound insights. It's like the best movie ever. You don't know what's going to happen, but you feel really connected to the characters, and there's always a surprising plot twist in the end.

A couple of years ago, the founders of a new high-efficiency engine design company contacted me about one of their difficult employees. The founders were Russian immigrants, graduates of MIT, highly intelligent physicists and engineers. While their employee, Geoff, was highly skilled in a very rare and hard-to-find expertise, they bluntly stated, "If he doesn't change, he's fired. And he knows this." Apparently, Geoff was arrogant, impossible to work with and the cause of other quality engineers leaving the company. While they admitted he was the smartest guy on the team, with a specific and hard-to-find type of technical expertise, they were going to have to fire him if he didn't change. The company was backed by venture capital firms who were putting pressure on them to move quicker, but with Geoff refusing to work well with others and regularly pissing people off to the point of storming out of the office, he'd become a huge liability.

To my surprise, when I called Geoff for our initial intake conversation, he was more than willing to come to NYC and spend four days working with me. "I know that they are not happy with me," he said, in reference to his two bosses. I asked, "Are you happy with you?" "Yes," he said. "Do you want to stay with the company?" "Yes," he said. "So you're willing to come work with me?" I asked. "I'm interested in anything that has to do with the mind. I'm interested in learning. So, yes. I'm willing. And if it keeps me from getting fired, that would be good, too." While his statements were open and willing, his feeling was quite cold and mechanical.

When Geoff showed up at my office in Manhattan a couple of weeks later to begin the program, I was absolutely shocked that he was my age, early thirties. I had assumed, by his voice and the way he spoke to me, that he was in his 50s. I'd never heard such a stiff, serious 30 year-old. In our first meeting, I got out a sketchpad and a couple of colored pens. As I said, sometimes I'll draw pictures as we're talking about the principles because visuals can be useful. We'd barely said our hellos to one another, and he looked at me blankly and said, "What is this, kindergarten? Are we going to color together?" The edginess in his voice made me bristle for a second, but then I relaxed and I said, "Actually, it would be amazing if you could be like a kindergartner over the next few days. Don't be an expert. Don't be super smart. Just hang out like you don't know anything about life yet. And yeah, sometimes we'll color together because pictures can be useful, but mostly we'll just talk. The general rule is, the more open you are, the more you'll get out of this experience. You can't learn something new if you think you already know everything. And kindergarteners are great at knowing nothing and being comfortable with it." I could see him shift in his chair. He was surprised by the quickness of my response. He didn't make me uncomfortable, which I think surprised him, as I later learned he's not used to people liking him much. And I saw that he heard the truth in what I said. Kindergarteners do make good learners, and he knew it. So we were off to a surprisingly good start!

While Geoff and I worked together over four days, dialoguing about the mind, there were several profound moments where Geoff's reality seemed to crack a bit, and new light was able to come in. He'd always been incredibly brilliant. He'd been inventing things since he was a young child. In spite of his robust mind, he'd never been able to work well with others. He found other people's thinking and behavior limiting to him, yet he knew he had to work with others to innovate large scale projects like the alternative energy engine he was currently a part of designing. He openly felt that his thinking was superior to others', so he found it difficult to tolerate other people and work together on projects. We discussed the fact that everybody sees the world through the lens of their own thinking, and because consciousness makes our thinking feel real in our body, almost all of us tend to think we're *right*. Because we feel right to ourselves. It doesn't mean we *are* right, or that we want to treat other people as if their thinking is irrelevant. At this point, Geoff and I had a great rapport, and I felt like he was direct and transparent with me, and I was with him. He said to me at one point, "If I have a vision for progressing on a project that I believe in, I don't think other people's thinking or feelings are relevant. I don't think people are relevant *period* if you have a clear vision that you know is right." I listened to him silently. I stared into his eyes. As he said this, there was so much arrogance and so little compassion for the humanity and the intelligence of other people in his tone. Without any judgment – because honest to goodness, I'd developed a strong rapport with Geoff, I actually really liked him – as I listened to him say that, the thought floated into my head, "I imagine that's how Hitler felt." I didn't say it out loud. I just sat there looking at him. And then he said, after a few moments of silence, "I sound like Hitler right now, don't I?" My jaw silently fell open. Did he actually just *say* what I had thought a moment before? "You said it. Not me," I said with a smile on my face. I didn't think it wise to draw comparisons between a client and Hitler, but if he said it himself, then by all means! I couldn't believe it. It was really true, and he suddenly saw it in himself. If you put a commitment to your own ideas over other human beings, you become a fundamentalist, or a raging psycho, and nobody likes you. Suddenly he was interested. "I don't want to be like Hitler," he said. "Yeah, he's not a very popular guy," I said. "And look what happened to his vision. It didn't work out so well. The thing is, you're obviously a far cry from Hitler, but you *are* bringing out the worst in the people on your team by not caring about them, not seeing the inherent value in them and not being interested in their ideas. Has it ever occurred to you that you could be a catalyst for bringing out the best in them, and then you guys might move quicker toward your goal? As it stands right now, your arrogance is slowing down the whole team." I could see that the dominoes were falling. He'd never considered how much *he* might be the one limiting things. He'd always assumed it was everyone else that was the problem.

After our "Hitler" conversation, we took a break for lunch. Geoff went wandering around the city on his own. When he came back for our afternoon meeting, he looked different. He was visibly lighter and more pleasant. He explained to me that he'd gone to a diner for lunch and had a really interesting new experience. "I just went to an average diner. I like those places. And in walked several policemen. I don't like the police. As an institution, I don't like them. I don't think they're an intelligent group of people, for the most part. But as I sat there eating my sandwich, I realized how much of my bad feeling about cops came from this thinking that I have about them that I think is so true and important. So I just experimented with letting it go. Not focusing on it. Not spending my whole lunch staring at them and thinking about how much I hate police. And it was really cool because as I let that go, I found they just became human beings. They weren't *cops,* they were just people. And I started to feel a lot of warmth toward them. They looked like they were having a really nice time together. They seemed like nice people. And by the time I finished my sandwich and left, I liked them. I had an experience of liking cops. That's pretty new for me," he said with a genuine smile on his face. He was becoming a kindergartener in the best way. He was becoming open and new thought was coming in. Over the remainder of our few days working together, Geoff continued to get more humble, more open and genuinely interested in how that space of mind would allow him to have different outcomes with people. He had uncovered why relationships with people had always been a source of difficulty in his life, and even more exciting for someone like Geoff, he had discovered that caring about them was actually a vital piece of success in innovation. He could now go back to work knowing how to collaborate with people from within his own mind. And *that* would lead to the results he wanted.

I found it touching and surprising that a couple weeks after he went back to work in Connecticut, I received a book in the mail from Geoff. It was *Journey To Ixtlan,* by Carlos Castanedas. On the opening page were the quotes of praise for the book. The final quote read, *"It is impossible to view the world in quite the same way."* - Chicago Tribune. Scrawled in black pen was an arrow pointing to that quote and a personal note from Geoff that read,

"Hi Mara, I hope that someday they're saying this about your book. Thanks for the time you spent with me, I enjoyed it... Geoff."

Like I said, Geoff was not a particularly warm person when I initially met him, so to receive a gift from him in the mail with such kind and encouraging words warmed my heart.

As can sometimes happen, I tried without success to follow up with his bosses in the weeks and months after I worked with Geoff. They had gotten caught up in seeking another round of funding and kept canceling or postponing our follow up calls. I knew from talking to Geoff, that he was very happy back at work, but I had no idea what his bosses would say (other than obviously, they hadn't fired him). Almost exactly one year to the day after Geoff completed his program with me, I received an email out of the blue from his bosses while I was on vacation on a lake in Canada. As I sat on the deck overlooking the beautiful lake, I was overwhelmed with a sense of delight as I read their Russian physicist's version of a gushy email: *I'd like to report that we are seeing enormous positive changes in Geoff - he is our star employee now! Hope you could do the same for us. How does your schedule look for me and the other co-founder to both attend your program?* Star employee!? Geoff had become their star employee. I gasped and laughed.

To make a long story short, I was delighted to then work with Geoff's two bosses. One of whom is a whole other story for another day. He actually cried during one of our meetings and said, "As a physicist raised in communist Soviet Union, I never thought I'd say this...but I feel connected to something deeper and more spiritual than just me and the hard, cold facts of science. I never thought I would feel this way in my lifetime. I didn't know there was anything else."

Nine

My Dad's Story, Written by Kevin Gleason

*"Going twice as far in half the time with half
the effort lies in the power of the mind."*

- Kevin Gleason

I thought I was doing everything right. Things were rolling along in my life, and I thought I was doing pretty well as a husband, a father, a newly appointed CEO, and just an all-around human being. In my opinion, my mental state was pretty good for a guy who was supporting a family with three kids and operating a company of over 400 employees. The challenges I was experiencing in being a father, a husband and a boss, and the stress associated with these responsibilities, seemed like a natural by-product of the life I was living.

It seemed OK to me that my relationship with my wife was strained because that's the way most relationships were at the time. I didn't know many people in my situation, knee deep in family and career, who were experiencing healthy, happy and robust marriages. As far as parenting went, I knew I was making mistakes but blamed my shortcomings as a father on outside circumstances that would eventually change as things settled down, and I would have more time and patience to devote to the kids. I just needed more balance on the home front, and things would get better.

At work, my adrenalin was always pumping with the excitement of growing the business. With that excitement often came the frustration of seeing things move too slowly, which I couldn't understand. Where was the sense of urgency? Why were people so mired in the process and less focused on the outcomes? As a result, I became a pusher. I constantly challenged employees to do more, to work with a greater sense of urgency and collaborate with their peers without so much fucking drama. It seemed the harder I pushed, the more pushback I received, which only led to stress and frustration for me and for those around me. I felt strongly that my vision for the company was the right vision, my ideas the right ideas, and it was emotionally draining to face so many obstacles in my pursuit of managing a profitable company. There was constant tension in the work environment, a culture of uneasiness that was like an electrical current in the office. We were a productive company, more than most, I thought, but the toll was significant. In essence, it was a highly productive operating model that was highly dysfunctional. Employees were always on edge because I was always on edge. My family was always on edge because I was always on edge. What I really wanted was an operating model in life that would allow me to go twice as far in half the time, with half the effort.

Something I didn't recognize at the time, something entirely invisible to me but ironically at the core of all of my dysfunction and unhappiness, was that I was angry. I was pissed off, and for the life of me, I couldn't tell you why or where it came from. I had achieved more than I ever thought possible, but for some reason, this feeling of animosity was very real to me and permeated my emotional landscape. It manifested itself in many ways but most frequently appeared as chronic frustration with people and circumstances, resulting in my being a difficult guy to get along with. I lacked patience and was too condescending and abrasive with folks for no real reason.

I was mad at my wife for not loving me more and not being more supportive. I was mad at my kids for knowing how they felt about me, knowing I made them uneasy the moment I walked in the door because they never knew which of my moods they were about to experience. When they were younger, they couldn't wait for Dad to show up, but somehow things had changed over time.

I was mad about things at work. This or that person was conspiring to undermine all of the hard work and effort we were putting forth as an organization, and as soon as you would fire one person, another would pop up and take his place. The people who were putting forth the effort were inconsistent in their approach. Why couldn't they just do their damn job? Who wouldn't be upset, right?

The amazing thing at the time was my total lack of awareness of how my anger was playing footsie with my state of mind. Today, when I look back on those times, I realize that my complete lack of understanding of the relationship between my state of mind and the impact it was having on my thinking was the root of all the problems I was experiencing. Anger was like my skin; it was as much a part of me as anything. It was almost as if this feeling of anger was a genetic trait, a predisposition in my DNA, like height or hair color. My father had it, as did his father, and we were unknowingly handing it down from generation to generation. In my mind, I didn't know I had any choice in how I felt, but as I later came to realize, that couldn't have been further from the truth.

This is the story of how a weekend trip to La Conner, Washington, in 1991 and my initial exposure to the three principles began a process of allowing me to experience life in a very different way. It was a launch pad in a life-altering journey of gaining a deeper insight into my psychological functioning that to this day allows me a deeper and richer appreciation for my moment-to-moment experiences, providing me the opportunity to enjoy life more than I ever thought possible. Funny thing is, it wasn't that difficult.

But let's start with why I was going to La Conner in the first place …

Rewind the tape back to 1991.

The economy was in a recessionary environment, and the outdoor advertising company I managed was having difficulty meeting our debt obligations. We had too much leverage, and the lending institutions were becoming increasingly concerned about our ability to service debt. Among the various options being explored was the possibility of putting the company into default and selling the assets, essentially putting us out of business. The other option was less draconian, allowing us to restructure the debt, extend the amortization and have a window of time to improve performance and achieve certain income expectations. We were given six months. The debt at the time was around $300 million. Every employee knew we were on the bubble and realized the six-month fuse had been lit. We also knew we had one shot to make it and wouldn't be given a second chance.

So what were we going to do and how were we going to do it? What happened next changed my life forever. Looking back, it's interesting how in the most challenging times one can imagine, the most unimaginable things happen.

I was in my office in Atlanta one day when Steve, the owner of the company, called me and suggested taking our senior management team out to Washington State for a "wellness weekend": a retreat, of sorts, where we could get a brief reprieve from the stress of our current situation. A fellow named George Pransky would host the event at the community center in downtown La Conner, a fishing and tourist village just north of Seattle. Needless to say, I was astounded and thought the recommendation absurd. As a company, we had less than six months to achieve cash flow obligations, meet bank expectations and prove that we were capable of meeting our debt service, or it was lights out. How was it possible that we were even considering such an irresponsible action? Doing some quick math in my head, I calculated the cost to be around $100,000 to fly our leadership team to a remote town in the Northwest for a three-day "wellness retreat." What kind of bullshit was this? We didn't have the time or the money for this nonsense. The problem was, I didn't own the company, and for some reason unknown to me, the owner was adamant. We were going to La Conner. So off we go, and after three days in La Conner I can honestly tell you my feet were firmly planted in midair.

George Pransky was a Colombo-like character. Kind of bumbling, kind of funny, low key with a graceful approach to his manner and a thoughtfulness to his delivery. He was a curious individual that I had difficulty drawing a bead on, but the moment he started talking, I felt a heightened sense of being OK and a lessening in my discomfort of being there when I thought I should have been elsewhere. The meeting room was a charming town hall space where I began to feel pretty relaxed, kicking back and listening to George talk about these principles behind life, and against my better judgment, I found myself enjoying the day. After the meeting, my wife and I took a stroll around town and found that it, too, was quite charming, with a waterway and a saltwater slough actually running through the middle into Puget Sound. There was a beautiful orange-reddish colored bridge at the end of town that gave La Conner an almost otherworldly look, which was most fitting because I was about to be transported into another world, another reality.

One Thought Changes Everything

As day one drifted into day two and day two became day three, I felt myself slowing down, deepening, becoming more introspective and gaining more perspective in my mind about life, in general. The world I had been trapped in prior to my visit to La Conner didn't seem so daunting, so overwhelming, and I was enjoying my physical and social context more than I had in quite some time. There's a line in a song that says, "The more you have, the less you see." Well, without knowing it, I was beginning to see more because I had less on my mind, and I was more open to the beauty of all things around me than I had been three days ago. It's kind of what people used to call a "natural high." But more importantly, something else was happening that, once again, I couldn't put my finger on. Unbeknownst to me, I wasn't so angry.

It's important to note here that much of what George was saying was difficult for me to comprehend. My opinions of life and how I related to my situation were in stark contrast to George's ideas on one's life experience. I struggled at first, and I could sense that others were in the same situation. But as we got deeper into the conversation, I realized that there was a tug of war happening between my intellect and my feelings. Intellectually, I was desperate to figure things out, and it was exhausting. Emotionally, I was feeling something at a deeper level, something I hadn't experienced in a long time, and it felt good. It was a feeling of comfort and reassurance. There was a voice, not in my head but in a deeper dimension, telling my brain to slow down, calm down, and things would make sense without my having to work so hard.

I really didn't understand what was happening, but it was very noticeable to me that my feeling state had changed and in a most wonderful way. I couldn't articulate what was going on because words were failing me dramatically in my ability to explain this phenomenon to myself or others. I knew it had something to do with my mind slowing down and the principles that George was talking about, but I couldn't put my finger on much more than that. Ironically, I didn't have to wait long, as help was on the way. As the three days drew to a close, and just as I was about to leave La Conner, George approached me and suggested I return in two weeks for "further counseling." Needless to say, I was conflicted because I was responsible for spearheading the restructuring of the company back home and really didn't have the time. "Let me do what I need to do back home, and I promise to return in six months or so" was my response. Yet there was another part of me that wanted to continue this exploration of what was happening because something wonderful was definitely affecting my experience, and for the life of me, I couldn't tell where it was coming from. But reality set in, and my thoughts about the restructuring were too overwhelming, and I decided I needed to focus on business and delay my return. I explained this to George, as politely but firmly as possible, only to realize George had something else in mind.

George sat me down, looked me in the eye and told me that he was concerned. He was concerned that my leadership "style" was too harsh, too abrasive and even though productive, was short term in nature and came at too high of a price to myself and those around me. It was unacceptable to choose this path when a wiser path was available, and we just needed time together to see the truth of what he was saying. Before I could offer any resistance, he indicated he had spoken to Steve, the owner of the company, and this is what had been decided.

Every person has defining moments in life, and for me, this was one of them. "We seldom have any clue that a life-changing event is waiting in the wings. The experience that was to forever change my life and career was about to happen." (Sydney Banks, *The Enlightened Gardener*).

Fast forward two weeks, and once again I am in La Conner with George, but this time one-on-one, mano-à-mano. No one else from the company came back with me.

I arrived at George's office and looked around, noticing how simple and undistracted it was without the typical bookshelves, wall diplomas and other accoutrements of one's professional accomplishments. Just three chairs and a couple of nice windows overlooking a courtyard. George had invited an associate, Christine, to join us and asked if that was OK, to which I responded something like, "the more the merrier" as I was a little nervous, not really knowing what to expect.

After a brief moment of welcoming, George looked at me and said, "Tell me about your father. What kind of man was he?" There it was, I thought, the typical Freudian psychobabble question setting the groundwork for blaming my parents for all my issues. "Really? Is this the direction we're heading?" I thought. But hey, this wasn't my idea to begin with, so I'll just play along and see where it takes us. Lunch wasn't that far off.

"What would you like to know?" I replied.

"On a scale of one to ten, ten being the worst, how angry was your father?" George asked.

Bam. Silence filled the room. All of a sudden, my thoughts were jumpstarted by memories of my dad, and my feelings started to turn in a mysterious direction. A psychological rug had been pulled out from under me, and I was groping for traction. Collecting my thoughts and wanting to appear unaffected, I responded by asking George what he meant, to which he replied, "You know, how angry was your dad, on a scale of one to ten?"

I told George and Christine about my dad and what a wonderful man he was. That he could be the most loving and thoughtful father in the world, but at the same time, was strict in his own way because that's what parenting was like back then. My father loved me, and I knew that, but he also scared the hell out of me, like most dads of that generation. George went deeper with his questioning, and we talked for about twenty minutes or so on my relationship with my father, at which point he asked me for my number. As I was considering the answer, I realized that I had become much more relaxed and introspective, less nervous. I appreciated the calming effect George was having on my state of mind, as it allowed me to consider the topic without getting overly emotional or defensive. In other words, I had become receptive. Also, and even more significant, I had become reflective.

"He was tough, but it was offset by his love for me," I responded. "I'd give my dad a four on the anger meter."

George then asked Christine what she thought, and to my surprise, she gave my dad a nine, indicating she thought he was very angry. George chuckled and said, "That's interesting. I'd give him about a 14!"

I was shocked. I was mad. I was fascinated. I didn't know what to think. I just sat there.

Also, the fact that George was finding humor in all of this was putting me off a little. George went on to tell me that in his opinion, the environment I grew up in was overly harsh. Love didn't have to be paired with anger in order to raise well-meaning children, and due to these circumstances, I saw anger as life's norm. The reason I didn't see it as a factor in my life was that I just didn't see it; it was invisible. George went on to describe how my inability to see it gave me the ability to behave in a harsh and abrasive manner without understanding the negative and ill effects it had on others. I didn't see it as harsh and abrasive, having been accustomed to this emotional behavior all of my life. It was my blind spot.

At that moment, I had an epiphany and realized at a deeper level what George was saying, and a dimension of truth began to envelop me. I felt, as well as understood, the consequence of my behavior and the damage it was having on my family, my colleagues and on the human race in general. It was a feeling that drove past my intellect to a more thoughtful and reflective place, one closer to wisdom than intelligence. A feeling of despair came over me, and I looked up at George and said, "I'm fucked, aren't I? How can a life of honing this behavior over forty years be reconciled? How can I ever undo the damage I've done?"

Once again, George chuckled.

"That's easy," he said. "Now that you see it for what it is, we can fix it. It'll take about 20 minutes. But first, let's go have lunch, because I'm starving."

Walking off to grab some lunch, I'm wondering what George could possibly have up his sleeve that would fix me in 20 minutes. At the same time, I was feeling really, really good. I was relaxed and optimistic, looking forward to the afternoon.

Although it may have taken more like an hour, that afternoon George introduced me to the three principles more in depth. It was the beginning of my journey into a world of greater clarity and insight into how I manufacture my reality and how my life is defined by that reality. A world guided by three simple principles: mind, consciousness, and thought, that are the foundation of every person's experience of life. In exploring these principles, I realized for the first time that life wasn't coming to me from the outside, in but rather from the inside, out – and I was the creator of that life. George and I discussed the nature of thought and how people can get trapped in their own thinking: how the mind is limitless in its ability to sponsor new thought. The mind is a world of pure potential waiting to open new doors of wisdom and intelligence to those looking for answers. In essence, I didn't have to think the thoughts I was thinking. I had the option to parachute into a different world of understanding, a world not bound by the past. Free at last, free at last. I felt the weight of the past begin to lift, and a feeling of gratitude flushed through my system as I thanked George for giving me this gift of understanding.

One Thought Changes Everything

When I returned home to Atlanta, I gathered the family and told them of my transformative experience in La Conner. I explained to them that I now saw things in a new light and asked them to forgive me for my past behavior, knowing that things wouldn't be perfect, but that I would do the best I could to be a better father, a better person.

Over the next several months, I found that everything I knew and felt had somehow changed; somehow things were different. By reflecting with George over those three days about the principles and how the nature of this understanding plays out in our daily experience of life, I felt a deepening. I had begun my journey into understanding the relationship between thought and one's state of mind, and how the nature of thought has the power to tap into human potential in a most magnificent way. I learned that humans are thinking creatures. We are constantly thinking and have the capacity for enormous bandwidth in our thinking minds. Some thought is memory based, what the intellect already knows because of something that's been learned or experienced. Some thought isn't. Some thought is new and comes from the unknown, a place we haven't discovered through memory or experience. This realm of the unknown is where pure potential exists, waiting for us to discover new ways to live, to behave, to solve problems, to experience joy, to think. Every human being has this at his fingertips and it's absolutely free. It doesn't cost a dime. We are born with it. How does one change his or her mind? By changing his or her thought. It's that simple. Not to be confused with controlling your thinking by controlling your thoughts; it's just the opposite. It's the freedom to let a thought go, let ourselves go, be less defensive and let new thinking thrive in an environment of mental exploration.

Everyone has the capacity to change the way they think about life if there is a compelling reason to do so. One hundred percent of the time, this comes from inside the mind, not outside. Oftentimes, we think that circumstances dictate our reality, that our lives and our experience of life is shaped by the world around us as an outside-in experience. I have learned that this is not the case. Circumstances do not shape our experience of life; we do. Each one of us, every minute of every day, has the ability to shape and experience our reality from a more profound place, a deeper dimension, a more human place. I realized that I live in an inside-out world, shaped by my thinking and my state of mind.

I've realized that a person's state of mind is a barometer of their ability to access their inherent intelligence. If state of mind is a continuum and one end is healthy and the other end unhealthy, the closer one is to an unhealthy state of mind, the less opportunity for insight. It's hard to be a productive, creative thinker when the problems of the world are stressful and weigh on you. The healthier one's state of mind, the more reflective one becomes, lowering defenses and trusting in their ability to gain new insights by drawing on their own inherent intelligence. I firmly believe that when a person is in a reflective state, they are in a receptive state. A person in a receptive state is more open to new thought, and new thought brings about a world of possibilities.

So what did all this have to do with selling billboards? A hell of a lot, actually. When Steve, the company owner, decided we should all go to La Conner and visit with George at a time when our business was on the verge of collapse, he must have known what he was doing.

Fast forward 25 years.

Our company is now the fourth largest in our particular field in the United States. We have a healthy and robust relationship with our lenders and are regarded as the most profitable and best-managed company in the industry by Wall Street. Recently, we partnered with an investment firm to acquire another advertising company resulting in our doubling size.

It's my firm belief that the three principles are the "secret sauce" behind the success of our company. It is the key discriminator in our success. Let me explain. Revenues in our company are generated when a salesperson and a prospective client come together and transact a piece of business that allows the client to promote their product or service in our media. Our media, which is Out of Home (OOH), is in competition with all other traditional media forms, such as television, radio, cable, print and the Internet for advertiser dollars. As a result, we must be relevant to an advertiser's needs and provide strong return on investment (ROI) to our clients. Most think that selling media is about promoting values and benefits. On the contrary, selling media is about delivering on an advertiser's goals by delivering on our ROI promise. What's always been curious to me is that all of us in media basically speak the same language and make the same promises, but who really delivers on that promise? Most are so busy promoting the value of their medium over others, the advertiser's goals are often overlooked in favor of shortening the sales cycle.

Those that deliver on the promise must understand what the goals are for the advertising investment. To understand those goals, one needs to get inside the mind of the advertiser and discover what's truly important. To do this, we must go beyond the presentation phase and explore the thinking of the client to better understand their world and how that world was created. In my opinion, there are two levels of existence: the known and the unknown. Our company operates in both worlds but favors the world of the unknown when working with clients. The unknown is a world of pure potential, a world waiting to be discovered where a shift in thinking can create new insights into campaign and media strategy. What does a client value, and what do they expect from their investment? Is it just about reaching a certain audience at a certain time with a certain message, or is there something more, something that will help them attain their goals and grow their business beyond the usual norm? In simple terms, what is possible beyond the scope of what is currently known which, if discovered, can be a game changer? More often than not, it's not what we know that gets us to where we want to be, but what we *don't* know.

Over the past 25 years, I've brought the principles into the organization, talking to our management teams about the value of understanding psychological functioning and its relevance to everything we do. All client interaction is improved when one understands the nature of thought and its interplay with one's state of mind. It's not what the client "thinks" that is paramount, but what they *could* think if given the opportunity. What they think is the known, and what they *could* think is the unknown. To engage a client in a conversation and be truly interested in their potential to view the world differently is paramount to us. This is different from asking loaded questions directed towards a sale. It provides the client an opportunity to reflect on what they do and why they do it. And as I mentioned before, when a person is in a reflective state, they are in a receptive state. Not to outside input, but to their own innate wisdom, their own inner voice helping them better understand why they do what they do. This state of reflection promotes curiosity, and curiosity often opens doors to discovering a better way to do things. In comes the power of pure potential and the world of possibilities. Once you realize it's not an outside-in world but an inside-out world, you realize quickly that the old paradigm of chipping away at objections, the typical sales process, is fraught with stress and aggravation on both sides. Nobody wants to change the way they think unless a better thought comes along. We are in the business of helping better thoughts come along.

In closing, I would like to leave you with this: Sometimes just one thought can change a moment, and that moment can change a life. That's a truth for my clients, my employees, my family and me. I have grown to understand and appreciate the gift of this understanding and have utilized this gift to build a better life for myself and those around me. In retrospect, I now realize my anger was just thought that was invisible to me, and I had the power to see it for what it was and make a change. My realization that my experience wasn't happening *to* me, but rather coming *from* me, changed my life. I no longer wear anger like a skin. Sure, it visits me, but it's not cast upon me like I once thought. I'll never give up the fight, but I enjoy the challenges that life provides with much more grace and gratitude then ever before. The three principles, and the accompanying appreciation for the beauty of the dynamic between one's state of mind and the quality of one's thinking, provide me with a much richer and more potent operating platform. I now understand how to go twice as far in half the time with half the effort because I know that once again, we are all only one thought away from a better life. I may have begun this journey a skeptic, but I now *know* it is as simple as this: One thought can change everything. And an understanding of the principles gives you the key to that kingdom.

Ten

ONE THOUGHT CAN CHANGE THE WORLD

"Someday is just a thought."

- EIRIK OLSEN

Sitting on my living room couch at 11 years old, when I heard my father say, "Things are going to be different now," I had no way of knowing at the time that not only was that statement true, but it was like a portal into a different future for me. I would not be here today, doing this work and typing these words, if it weren't for that moment. Recently, I experienced another one of those moments, which coincidentally also took place on a living room couch, only this time in Oslo, Norway. For some reason, this time I knew almost right away that I was experiencing a *this changes everything* kind of moment. I could feel it in the exploding particles of my mind and the tingling, excited sensation in my body. And it all came from one simple thing my boyfriend, Eirik, said to me: "You know that *someday* is just a thought."

It was an early evening in December of 2015, and Eirik and I had been discussing a conference we wanted to co-host with himself, me, Aaron and George and Linda Pransky sometime in 2016. Eirik and I had been dating for just under a year, and while we'd originally met back in 2012 at a work related event, we hadn't put two and two together that we'd be perfect for each other until Linda Pransky stuck it under our noses. I'd always assumed, because he was five years younger and living in Norway, that it wasn't likely. I'll admit I'd always been curious about him. He stuck out as notably more attractive than the average conference attendee and undoubtedly intriguing due to his "Norwegianess." Embarrassingly, I had also made up that he probably only went for young, perfect-looking women, because he appeared young and perfect looking. This wasn't a thought I was conscious of at the time; it was more of a snap assessment that I could only see and admit to myself later.

I'd heard through the grapevine that he had been successful in bringing the principles-based understanding to Scandinavia, growing first his individual coaching and consulting practice, and later NorthMind, a company he started with three other colleagues. But that same "Norwegianess" that made him intriguing also worked against him, in that he never gave off any vibes of being curious about or interested in me. He rarely approached me or initiated conversation. When we bumped into each other a couple times per year at conferences or events, our interactions were always professional and brief. While I assumed there was no chemistry, I later learned that's just a cultural "flaw." It turned out Eirik was always curious about me, too, but Norwegians don't send women vibes like American men do. At least not as blatantly. I was used to knowing, rather quickly, if a guy was interested in me. Furthermore, he'd assumed I was off limits: either with a boyfriend or not interested in him. So, for our own silly, made-up reasons in our own heads, in the first few years of knowing each other, we had been blind to one other as a romantic possibility. While we couldn't see it, it turned out that Linda Pransky could. (For those who know Linda, this is a beautiful and irritatingly recurrent trait of hers.)

From the very beginning of my career, Linda and George were my teachers. George had been my father's teacher, and then both he and Linda had become close family friends and more or less watched me grow up from the age of 11 onward. As Linda tells it, she always had her eye on me. They had taken me on as a young intern right out of school, and even more, they'd taken me in like a family member. I felt like I got not only the best mentors on the planet, but also a second set of parents. They loved me like their own, and the feeling was mutual. Even after Aaron and I left Pransky and Associates to start our own company, One Thought, which could have been awkward or contentious, we stayed very close to them as friends, family and colleagues, often partnering on projects, advisory boards or conferences.

Linda and George later became Eirik's teachers. In 2013, Pransky and Associates launched a wider mentorship training program, drawing three principles professionals from all around the world. Prior to that, you had to be one of the lucky *very* few who got to do an internship with them, like Aaron and I did. But after 2010, the three principles field was expanding more rapidly than ever, especially outside the United States. While Aaron and I were busy with a full roster of international students each year on the One Thought Institute in London, George, Linda and their colleague Barb Patterson were in high demand with their new mentorship program in La Conner, Washington. The principles were a profound new way of understanding the human experience, and it was spreading like wild fire, with practitioner training institutes popping up all over the globe.

As I mentioned, one of the places it was spreading rapidly was in Scandinavia, in large part due to Eirik Olsen. After completing a year-long academy with one of the more widely known three principles coaches, Michael Neill, Eirik registered for the Pransky and Associates mentorship program. When I asked him recently what it was that drew him to their program, I was tickled, though not all that surprised, now that I know Eirik, by his reason. He said, "Because they didn't do much for me. When I first saw them present at one of the modules on Michael Neill's program, I wasn't very impressed or impacted. I couldn't understand what all the fuss was about." *Interesting. They didn't do much for you, so you signed up for their (not inexpensive) immersive six-month mentorship program that required frequent trips from Oslo, Norway, to northern Washington state.* This cracked me up in it's seeming ridiculousness. He said he was curious because he *knew* there must be something there, even if it wasn't immediately visible to him. They were widely respected and referenced, perhaps more than any other people in the field of the three principles besides Sydney Banks. But when Eirik first heard them present, he says he didn't really *get it*. Nothing they shared really resonated with him on a deep level. With so many practitioner training programs on offer all over the world, and certainly some closer to Oslo (ahem … the One Thought Institute in London, for example!), it was an unusual choice. Rather than pursue training with people he liked and *got*, Eirik thought it would be more interesting to go with the people he didn't. This is one of the many things I've grown to love and respect about Eirik. He often looks for what would be easy and obvious, and then consciously goes in the exact opposite direction because he knows it will be a richer experience. Now, he'll tell you, he absolutely made the right decision.

After completing the mentorship program with George, Linda and Barb, they recognized Eirik as a new, young, rising star in the field. They'd grown to love and respect him as a colleague and human being. In late October of 2014, Linda, my "second mom," watched me slowly flip-flop my way out of a dead-end relationship, and the second I had both feet out of it, she jumped on the opportunity to assist me in my love life. "What about Eirik? You know, Norwegian Eirik from our mentorship program? He's perfect for you, Mar. He's visionary. He's a leader. And he has tremendous depth. There's a lot of feeling there. He's really strong but really feeling-full. Actually, he's basically a male version of you. Seriously, why don't you go for him?"

I laughed, because I had literally broken up with my boyfriend the day before. I said, "OK, maybe. But can you give me a minute!? I have only been single for about 14 hours. Let me let the dust settle."

"OK," she said. And then two days later, she brought it up again. I could sense she wasn't going to let this one go. To make a long story short, Linda schemed and nudged over the next few months until she finally had us right where she wanted us: together in La Conner, Washington, at a training where she'd strategically hired me to present and she knew Eirik would be attending. We both fell into her perfectly laid trap, but the best part is, Eirik knew nothing of it. She never spoke a word to him about, "Why don't you go for Mara?" She'd only whispered in *my* ear, and yet when we were there in La Conner, it was Eirik who initiated things. While at an evening cocktail reception, he asked if I'd like to go sit outside on the patio and talk for a bit, as the fireplace was making the room quite hot and smoky. While it was most certainly true that the room was hot and smoky, it seemed entirely too coincidental. For days after, I thought *for sure* Linda had put him up to it. But both Linda and Eirik have sworn to me that he had no idea she had been scheming. He just realized, in that moment, that he wanted to get to know me more. And so we did: we went outside and got to know each other more, and inevitably discovered that we felt we'd already known each other for a very, very long time. In the weeks and months after that patio conversation, we fell quickly, deeply in love. Linda was right. We were perfect for each other.

OK. So, enough of the love story. Let's skip ahead to the living room couch in Oslo when we were kicking around ideas about a conference and then my mind exploded. It was essentially impossible for Eirik and I *not* to professionally collaborate, given that sharing the principles is always more of a calling or a passion than a job for those of us in the field. Eirik and I were in love but also in love with our "work." It was natural and unavoidable that we talked about our visions and ideas of how we could help more people in new ways. I loved that our dreams and visions were often as similar as they were totally different and that he had a fresh perspective. We knew that this understanding of the mind can shed new light on nearly every area of life, and it was exciting to kick around ideas about how to grow the positive impact in the world. One idea that we had both had, separately, was to host some kind of event that could make more of a direct impact on global issues. Throughout 2015, Aaron and I had been playing with an idea of launching a kind of executive leadership institute, where we would bring together senior leaders of organizations that we had worked with to learn together and consider business challenges as well as larger economic and global issues from a new vantage point, enabled by an understanding of the three principles. Many brilliant leaders that we had worked with over the years hungered for a network of other leaders that appreciated how radically different running a business was when you had an understanding of the inside-out nature of life.

Furthermore, these leaders often became inspired to get involved in sharing this understanding with more of the world, because it was evident this understanding was the cure for so many personal, organizational, social and global challenges. Once you see a new understanding of the mind, you can't help but see how that means a new understanding of nearly *everything* we're up to in life. I can't count the number of times I sat across from intelligent, successful people who said, "This is so simple, and yet nobody knows about this. Why doesn't everybody know this!? We have to change that!" I had always wondered if we could just gather up these intelligent, successful people in a single room and say, "Hey, let's do this. Let's put our heads together about how we can change the world by catalyzing a paradigm shift in understanding. If people, individually and collectively, understood that the world is created from the inside-out via thought, we could begin to create healthier, more peaceful, productive, stable societies." But like many exciting ideas we'd had over the years, we were somewhat stuck in the "planning" phase: designing it, talking to people about it. We were close, but nothing was actually materializing yet.

Eirik's idea was that he wanted to have a conference in Oslo and invite me, Aaron, George and Linda to be speakers, but rather than speak about what we usually speak about at conferences (which was the principles as an understanding that helps individuals, families and businesses), this conference would focus 100 percent on the principles as a solution to large-scale global issues: War. Poverty. Refugee crises. It seemed like it was time to elevate the conversation in our field to try to help an increasingly suffering world.

Rightly or wrongly, the world in 2015 seemed to be more and more in a fear-driven mode. The threat of terrorism, both domestic and foreign, loomed like a constant dark cloud. The seemingly endless instability in the Middle East, including the horrendous Syrian conflict, was (and still is) fueling the largest refugee crisis since World War II. Images of a dead Syrian refugee toddler washed up on the shores of Greece shocked the world. Racial tensions in America were on the rise as innocent black men continued to lose their lives to frightened police officers. Brexit. Trump v. Hilary. Twenty-four-hour media programs were pointing out the suffering, divide and conflict everywhere you looked.

Conversely, our work had been showing us over the years, client by client, family by family, organization by organization, that there is a simple understanding that actually shows how we're all the same. We're not divided. In fact, we're very much the same. All humans just want to feel OK. Period. End of story. But because we have different kinds of thinking and different thoughts we have made up, individually and collectively, about where our feelings of "OK" come from, there is a lot of suffering, instability and divide that doesn't need to be going on. Our field was illuminating a universal set of principles that explains a) where the human experience and feelings *actually* come from, and b) that we're all using the same basic principles to create our experience, so we're all the same underneath our separate thoughts. Those two facts, *if and when understood*, make the world immediately more united, stable and hopeful. In my career, I witnessed thousands of people begin to have insights into those facts and watched them become more peaceful about life and more able to sort out conflict. People often described it as putting on a new pair of prescription glasses when you'd had bad eyesight for years but didn't know it. Witnessing it so many times, in so many different kinds of people, I'd begun to walk around with the unique sense that anything and everything was solvable if people truly understood how the mind, and the world we have created for ourselves, truly works.

As Eirik and I sat on the couch discussing the conference about global issues, I felt myself getting more and more charged up.

"Yes!" I said. "I am so sick of watching the news or reading the papers and seeing all of the struggles of the world and thinking, *If only everyone understood how the mind really works, then none of this shit would be happening. There's actually a really simple solution.* You can't have racism if you know that everything is made of thought. Racism isn't a *thing*. It's a thought that someone treats as though it's true. Babies aren't racist because they haven't learned to believe that their thinking is correct yet and no one has taught them the ridiculous *thought* that skin color implies anything other than different pigment, just like different hair color. And you can't have war because you could never kill someone if you knew that we all live in our own thought-created, separate realities. And to say that mine is right and yours is wrong makes no sense. Or to blame someone else or some group of people for *making me* feel something stops making sense. How could I harm someone if they can't make me feel bad? Even the lines we've drawn around territories and states and countries. They're all made of thought. And then we argue over them like they somehow exist outside of thought. It's crazy.

"**Someday**," I continued, "everyone will understand these principles and then, and only then, will the world actually experience peace and global security!"

Eirik looked at me, totally dead-pan, and said, "You know that *someday* is just a thought, too. It doesn't exist. It's just an idea. So it never gets any closer."

And that's when my head exploded.

Every time I've ever had a moment of insight where I've seen, in a nanosecond, the illusion -- the absolute, complete and utter made-upness of something in my existence that I had previously taken to be real -- there's always a series of clicks that occur in my mind. Like a domino effect. Or a momentary "life flashing before your eyes." Not like the way it does when you have a close encounter with death, but literally I sort of go back through my life and *click ... click ... click,* the truth gets plugged in where there had previously been illusion. It was the same feeling when I realized my father didn't cause my bad feelings; my thinking about him did. In that tiny but massive moment of insight while cooking rice in my kitchen, I did a five-second retrospective of my entire childhood and saw *all* the times I'd blamed him for my bad feeling and instead, I now saw myself thinking about him in a painful way. My childhood went from a series of events *caused* by him, to a series of events generated by my own mind. In that moment when Eirik said, "You know, 'someday' is just a thought," the same flash occurred. I realized about fifteen things in the flash of a second. One was that time is an illusion. Period. We only experience now. I know people talk about that all the time, and I know I had glimpsed that notion several times before, but in that moment I felt the truth of it in my entire being. *Someday is made up. It's just a thought. It's not a real thing. Therefore, there's no such thing as 'someday' people realizing the principles underlying human existence that will 'someday' solve these chronic, tragic, problems.*

"Oh my god. You're right. We just have to do this now."

"Exactly," Eirik said. "It's not something for later. No one else is going to do it. It's not just going to happen. If we see it, we should do something about it now. That's the only true space in which anything ever happens. Otherwise, it just stays in the land of ideas and never gets any closer."

The other thing I realized is that I had based my entire career on a *someday gets you closer to now* premise, and I realized how profoundly wrong I was. Somewhere along the line without my realizing it, the sneaky invisible idea crept into my mind and took hold that you have to build up to doing what you really want to do in life. You have to take steps. Build credibility. Gain *permission,* diligently, over time, to then be able to do your *someday* dream. *Someday* we'll be sharing these principles with global leaders and helping to stop wars that fuel refugee crises, violence, economic disparity, etc. *Someday* we'll be talking with the lead thinkers on reversing climate change to help them see that greed and overconsumption are really at the crux of environmental degradation and none of that would exist if people didn't need more money, and convenience, and bigger and *more* in order to feel good in life. In the words of my new colleague, Stephanie Fox, "If human beings actually started to just use what they need, instead of what they *think they need* in order to feel good." Someday the United Nations and other global organizations will realize that dealing with the symptoms of our problems is like painting over the cracks in the walls of a shoddy house. The source of all global issues is the human misunderstanding of thought. We have to go to the source if we want to make real and lasting headway on any issue. In that moment, I saw that I had a million and one *somedays,* and none of them were ever going to get any closer to reality. If I wanted to make something happen, I had to see it and do it now. Goddamn, it felt amazing to realize that! Because in that moment, I realized that the only thing standing in my way was the illusion of my own thinking. Yup. That thing again! Once you see it for what it is, the jig is up. The realness of your own ideas dissolves into thin air, and then you're suddenly free to play outside of those walls.

After that moment, we decided right then and there that we would have a conference dedicated to showing that an understanding of the mind would solve all major global issues, and we would do our best to get the right audience for the message. How successful we were was irrelevant. It was about setting our sights on a new direction and doing the best we possibly could to deliver something profoundly new and hopeful to whomever was willing to listen.

I remember the final moment of that conversation on the couch was when I said, "So when should we aim for? Like, a year from now?"

And Eirik said, "No, that's too long. Let's do it in May."

"MAY!" I said. "But that's so soon! That's less than five months away. I don't know that we'll be ready by then."

"Babe," he said. "We're never going to feel ready. Ready is just another thought. Let's just do it."

I smiled and felt equal parts giddy and terrified.

"OK," I said. "Let's do it in May."

That was the beginning of what I now think of as our crazy magic carpet ride. For the next five months, we hustled and planned and cold-called and reached out to every last contact we had to see who would be interested in attending a conference that we had boldly decided to call One Solution. We wanted to prove a seemingly impossible hypothesis that any world problem would look solvable if people really understood how the mind was the real (and only) source of that problem, and how the mind *actually* worked: from the inside-out, not outside-in. Step one: see the *actual source* of an issue (not just get lost in the symptoms). Step two: understand that source so that you can make change.

It was wildly simple and yet hard for many people to comprehend. However, I found it the most heartening and encouraging experience to speak to people about the vision for the conference, because most people -- certainly not all, but most

-- were receptive and hopeful upon hearing it. It's hard for me to wrap my head around it, but in that brief, five-month period of unabashedly putting our message out to the world and not waiting for *someday*, I managed to shake hands on a stage with Sir Richard Branson of Virgin, have lunch with Scilla Elworthy, humanitarian and one of the creators of the Elders, have lunch with Eason Jordan of CNN and the Malala Fund, have phone calls and meetings with dozens of other change-makers, and get to know, and now consider friends, a UN program director in Africa who came to speak at the conference, and a passionate former UN refugee worker who now works alongside me at One Solution, our global nonprofit organization. All of those moments and the ripples that ensued were a result of one, new thought: *'someday' doesn't exist.*

I'm not going to lie. In the moments where I wasn't wildly excited and inspired, I was terrified and often frustrated with Eirik. I felt like he'd dragged me into something bigger than I could handle, and he had a ridiculous (in my opinion, of course) disregard for appearances. He was completely disinterested in anything that distracted us from the higher vision: *there is a solution to the world's problems.* Any sort of worrying about how the website looked, how well our newsletters read, whether or not our English and grammar were correct (which often weren't when written by a Norwegian) were a totally irrelevant waste of time, as far as he was concerned. I, on the other hand, was all too concerned about our critics. If someone said they thought something looked or sounded bad, I took it seriously. *Very seriously.* And plenty of people took it upon themselves to tell us how we were doing it wrong. The problem was that we didn't have enough time, or any budget, so to speak, to make anything perfect. Worrying about those kind of details was pointless. And really, even if we'd had oodles of time and a million-dollar budget, Eirik was (and is) never going to worry about those things because he doesn't feel that they matter. *Well!* With an Ivy League master's degree, and basically just a bunch of ego in my way, it was a lot for me to accept that we were just going to let unpolished, imperfect things go out into the world. However, with time (and one particular argument in a car) I came to realize that there's something beautiful about trusting that the truth of your message, your clarity and your sincerity are infinitely more powerful than your appearance. We later came to refer to it as the "umph" factor. "Umph" comes from the human spirit, and nowhere else. It's the truth of life, before we override it with all our ideas and thoughts about how things should look and what's right and wrong. "Umph" is undeniable. It resonates with all people. And it makes your stupid mistakes dim in contrast to its brightness. "Umph" is what we have continued to believe in and dig for and ultimately used to fuel the building of One Solution, the international NGO that now exists today.

As I stood on stage on May 22, 2016, at One Solution Oslo alongside Eirik, Aaron, George and Linda and took in the crowd of 200 or so people that were standing on their feet clapping, whistling and thanking us for the incredible conference we'd just concluded, I let myself go and just cried. I cried for so many reasons. I cried for gratitude that they heard us.

That we weren't crazy. That there really is one solution to all the world's problems and that those 200 people, plus the hundreds more streaming online around the globe, heard and felt the simple hope of that statement. I cried for the amazing people who joined us to speak at the conference, including Simon Charters and John Oeching who flew from Nairobi to show that the three principles were helping address corruption in the Kenyan police force: the first UN-led initiative incorporating the three principles, and it was working! Including Mahima Shrestha from Nepal, who showed that understanding the three principles made her and the children she worked with feel more secure and more resilient in spite of surviving a devastating earthquake. Including Jack Pransky, who showed how one of the most violent and drug-ridden housing projects in the US became drug-free, homicide-free and healthy after the residents were empowered with understanding the principles behind their own minds. Including Stephanie Fox, who explained how war and refugee crises, which she knows all too well after spending five years working for the UN in Gaza, will only be solved by people realizing that global security comes from individual security, which can only come when people feel secure in understanding their own minds. Including Peter Wilson, former UN trade facilitator, and Tore Skatun, former UN Development Program director, who shared how an understanding of the principles made them realize that this understanding of the mind inoculates people to the stress, burnout and frustration that plagues the humanitarian field (or any other, for that matter). Both felt that this was the fundamental missing piece that was keeping the UN trapped in an inefficient model of endless meetings about problems after problems, never really understanding and addressing the real source or solution. Including Jacqueline Hollows, who showed how sharing the principles with prison inmates was not only rehabilitating the prisoners into mentally healthy, whole people, but so much so that they were becoming an *asset* instead of a liability to the prison system. In their newfound health and good spirits, the inmates from her programs were helping other prisoners and prison staff and even offering to repair prison infrastructure, like plumbing and electric issues.

I cried for all the volunteers that had poured in from every corner: Norway, New York, California, New Zealand, and more! The number of people that offered their time and energy, for nothing in return, was shocking to me. People believed in the hope and the promise of One Solution, and they were willing to give freely of themselves to help make it happen. I had never been on the receiving end of so much humanity all at once, and it took my breath away.

I cried for one of the delightful, unexpected outcomes of the conference, which was that the attendees said it made them not only want to go out and help the world, but for once, they really understood that they *could* and that it was *simple*. Immediately after that conference, so many grassroots projects sprung up that wouldn't have begun otherwise.

I cried for the *knowing*. It's so easy and tempting to have doubts in life, but when you get to sit in a moment of absolute *knowing* that you're pointed in the right direction; that you're being honest with yourself and the world; that you are doing *exactly* what you want to be doing; that you feel reconnected to a purity of spirit that you had as a child; being in that knowing, even for a moment, is so huge and so rare, you can't help but cry at the enormity of it. I cried for the feeling that maybe, just maybe, this could change the world far quicker than I had thought in my eleven years of doing this work. I cried because it was over (or it was just beginning, actually). Because I had never thrown myself into working so wholly, with so little idea of whether it would amount to anything, but standing up on that stage I could see that all that work was not for naught.

I cried for George, Linda and Aaron bringing me into their lives and under their wings, guiding me to learn these principles and then share my understanding in a way that resonated and made a difference in the world. Aside from my parents and siblings, those three people have shaped my life more than anyone, and in that moment in particular, if felt like a pretty amazing life. I owe them more that I can quantify.

And of course -- of course -- I cried for love. Eirik had opened my eyes to a new world. I was so grateful and so overwhelmed by how much I loved him in that moment, I could barely breathe. I cried because my world had changed. And if my world had changed, that meant *the* world could change.

One Solution is now a global nonprofit with projects and conferences all over the world bringing a universally understandable and applicable solution to all global problems. To learn more, go to www.onesolutionglobal.org *or follow One Solution Global on YouTube and Facebook, and Instagram @onesolglobal.*

Acknowledgements

I would like to thank Michael Neill and Mary Schiller for making sure this book got off of my laptop and out into the world. Your guidance, encouragement and skills made the publishing of this book possible. Michael, your consistent support made me get over my fears and overthinking. Lord knows how much longer I would've waited without you. And Mary, thank you for always giving of yourself and your editing and publishing skills. Additional shout out to the super talented Monica LoCascio for your publishing and distribution wisdom, as well as your desire to help humanity.

It's difficult for me to even know where to begin when thanking Aaron Turner, Linda Pransky, and George Pransky. These three people have done more for my personal well-being, my professional success and my life trajectory than I can put into words. Aaron, thank you for always seeing more in me than I saw in myself and for grabbing my hand and jumping into the unknown together. The seven years we built One Thought together were incredible. I have always felt you were a unique and rare kind of work soulmate that very few people get to find in life. George and Linda, thank you for being my teachers, my "second parents" and my best friends. You gave me wings. Let me simply say, I love you all. You have been the greatest gift. Thank you.

Thank you to so many of my mentors, friends, and life cheerleaders who have helped me on my journey: Alexis, Vanessa, Uncle Brian, Matt, Lila, Elizabeth, Dicken, Sandy, Keith, Kara, Erika, Cathy, Barb, Robert, Chana, Terry, Elsie, Judy, Don, Frank, "The Fast Crowd," Brynne, Bronwen, Hilary and so many more. You have all contributed so much, whether you know it or not.

Mom, Dad, Max and Callie…you're even more difficult to thank because you're so embedded in my soul, it's hard to see you and appreciate you wholly. I love you like the air I breathe, grateful to have it but almost unaware because you've always, always been there. I am so blessed to have a family that I consider my best friends and who have always supported me living my dream. And Max, the cover of this book is better than I could have imagined, thanks to you. For more beautiful art by Max go to www.maxgleason.com

Eirik, as if that last chapter wasn't already one big, gushy thank you letter to you, I'll just add one more thing: thank you for being my soul mate. You have literally awakened my soul in a way that has been overwhelmingly beautiful and surprising. We were meant to be together. I know it.

And thank you to Sydney Banks for realizing and articulating the true source of world peace in the human mind. Your flame burns brightly in all of us and continues to spread across the world.

Printed in Great Britain
by Amazon